The Department of Energy

KNOW YOUR GOVERNMENT

The Department of Energy

Catherine Tuggle
and
Gary E. Weir

CHELSEA HOUSE PUBLISHERS

On the cover: A close-up view of photovoltaic cells on the roof of Beverly High School in Beverly, Massachusetts.

Frontispiece: Workers install a component of the DOE's large coil test facility, which will test huge electromagnets used to carry out research on fusion.

Chelsea House Publishers
Editor-in-Chief: Nancy Toff
Executive Editor: Remmel T. Nunn
Managing Editor: Karyn Gullen Browne
Copy Chief: Juliann Barbato
Picture Editor: Adrian G. Allen
Art Director: Maria Epes
Manufacturing Manager: Gerald Levine

Know Your Government
Senior Editor: Kathy Kuhtz

Staff for THE DEPARTMENT OF ENERGY
Assistant Editor: Karen Schimmel
Deputy Copy Chief: Nicole Bowen
Editorial Assistant: Elizabeth Nix
Picture Researcher: Dixon & Turner Research Associates, Inc.
Assistant Art Director: Loraine Machlin
Senior Designer: Noreen M. Lamb
Production Coordinator: Joseph Romano

3 5 7 9 8 6 4 2

Library of Congress Cataloging-in-Publication Data
Tuggle, Catherine
    The Department of Energy / Catherine Tuggle and Gary E. Weir.
        p. cm.—(Know your government)
    Bibliography: p.
    Includes index.
    Summary: Surveys the history of the Department of Energy, describing its structure, current functions, and influence on United States Society.
    ISBN 0-87754-839-0
            0-7910-0887-8 (pbk.)
    1. United States. Dept. of Energy—Juvenile literature.
2. Energy policy—United States—Juvenile literature. [1. United States. Dept. of Energy. 2. Energy policy.] I. Weir, Gary E.
II. Title. III. Series: Know your government (New York, N.Y.)   89-7296
HD9502.U52T84 1989   CIP
353.87—dc20   AC

CONTENTS

KNOW YOUR GOVERNMENT

CHELSEA HOUSE PUBLISHERS

INTRODUCTION

Government: Crises of Confidence

Arthur M. Schlesinger, jr.

From the start, Americans have regarded their government with a mixture of reliance and mistrust. The men who founded the republic did not doubt the indispensability of government. "If men were angels," observed the 51st Federalist Paper, "no government would be necessary." But men are not angels. Because human beings are subject to wicked as well as to noble impulses, government was deemed essential to assure freedom and order.

At the same time, the American revolutionaries knew that government could also become a source of injury and oppression. The men who gathered in Philadelphia in 1787 to write the Constitution therefore had two purposes in mind. They wanted to establish a strong central authority and to limit that central authority's capacity to abuse its power.

To prevent the abuse of power, the Founding Fathers wrote two basic principles into the new Constitution. The principle of federalism divided power between the state governments and the central authority. The principle of the separation of powers subdivided the central authority itself into three branches—the executive, the legislative, and the judiciary—so that "each may be a check on the other." The *Know Your Government* series focuses on the major executive departments and agencies in these branches of the federal government.

7

The Constitution did not plan the executive branch in any detail. After vesting the executive power in the president, it assumed the existence of "executive departments" without specifying what these departments should be. Congress began defining their functions in 1789 by creating the Departments of State, Treasury, and War. The secretaries in charge of these departments made up President Washington's first cabinet. Congress also provided for a legal officer, and President Washington soon invited the attorney general, as he was called, to attend cabinet meetings. As need required, Congress created more executive departments.

Setting up the cabinet was only the first step in organizing the American state. With almost no guidance from the Constitution, President Washington, seconded by Alexander Hamilton, his brilliant secretary of the treasury, equipped the infant republic with a working administrative structure. The Federalists believed in both executive energy and executive accountability and set high standards for public appointments. The Jeffersonian opposition had less faith in strong government and preferred local government to the central authority. But when Jefferson himself became president in 1801, although he set out to change the direction of policy, he found no reason to alter the framework the Federalists had erected.

By 1801 there were about 3,000 federal civilian employees in a nation of a little more than 5 million people. Growth in territory and population steadily enlarged national responsibilities. Thirty years later, when Jackson was president, there were more than 11,000 government workers in a nation of 13 million. The federal establishment was increasing at a faster rate than the population.

Jackson's presidency brought significant changes in the federal service. He believed that the executive branch contained too many officials who saw their jobs as "species of property" and as "a means of promoting individual interest." Against the idea of a permanent service based on life tenure, Jackson argued for the periodic redistribution of federal offices, contending that this was the democratic way and that official duties could be made "so plain and simple that men of intelligence may readily qualify themselves for their performance." He called this policy rotation-in-office. His opponents called it the spoils system.

In fact, partisan legend exaggerated the extent of Jackson's removals. More than 80 percent of federal officeholders retained their jobs. Jackson discharged no larger a proportion of government workers than Jefferson had done a generation earlier. But the rise in these years of mass political parties gave federal patronage new importance as a means of building the party and of rewarding activists. Jackson's successors were less restrained in the distribu-

8

tion of spoils. As the federal establishment grew—to nearly 40,000 by 1861—the politicization of the public service excited increasing concern.

After the Civil War the spoils system became a major political issue. High-minded men condemned it as the root of all political evil. The spoilsmen, said the British commentator James Bryce, "have distorted and depraved the mechanism of politics." Patronage, by giving jobs to unqualified, incompetent, and dishonest persons, lowered the standards of public service and nourished corrupt political machines. Office-seekers pursued presidents and cabinet secretaries without mercy. "Patronage," said Ulysses S. Grant after his presidency, "is the bane of the presidential office." "Every time I appoint someone to office," said another political leader, "I make a hundred enemies and one ingrate." George William Curtis, the president of the National Civil Service Reform League, summed up the indictment. He said,

> The theory which perverts public trusts into party spoils, making public
> employment dependent upon personal favor and not on proved merit,
> necessarily ruins the self-respect of public employees, destroys the
> function of party in a republic, prostitutes elections into a desperate
> strife for personal profit, and degrades the national character by lower-
> ing the moral tone and standard of the country.

The object of civil service reform was to promote efficiency and honesty in the public service and to bring about the ethical regeneration of public life. Over bitter opposition from politicians, the reformers in 1883 passed the Pendleton Act, establishing a bipartisan Civil Service Commission, competitive examinations, and appointment on merit. The Pendleton Act also gave the president authority to extend by executive order the number of "classified" jobs—that is, jobs subject to the merit system. The act applied initially only to about 14,000 of the more than 100,000 federal positions. But by the end of the 19th century 40 percent of federal jobs had moved into the classified category.

Civil service reform was in part a response to the growing complexity of American life. As society grew more organized and problems more technical, official duties were no longer so plain and simple that any person of intelligence could perform them. In public service, as in other areas, the all-round man was yielding ground to the expert, the amateur to the professional. The excesses of the spoils system thus provoked the counter-ideal of scientific public administration, separate from politics and, as far as possible, insulated against it.

The cult of the expert, however, had its own excesses. The idea that administration could be divorced from policy was an illusion. And in the realm of policy, the expert, however much segregated from partisan politics, can

9

never attain perfect objectivity. He remains the prisoner of his own set of values. It is these values rather than technical expertise that determine fundamental judgments of public policy. To turn over such judgments to experts, moreover, would be to abandon democracy itself; for in a democracy final decisions must be made by the people and their elected representatives. "The business of the expert," the British political scientist Harold Laski rightly said, "is to be on tap and not on top."

Politics, however, were deeply ingrained in American folkways. This meant intermittent tension between the presidential government, elected every four years by the people, and the permanent government, which saw presidents come and go while it went on forever. Sometimes the permanent government knew better than its political masters; sometimes it opposed or sabotaged valuable new initiatives. In the end a strong president with effective cabinet secretaries could make the permanent government responsive to presidential purpose, but it was often an exasperating struggle.

The struggle within the executive branch was less important, however, than the growing impatience with bureaucracy in society as a whole. The 20th century saw a considerable expansion of the federal establishment. The Great Depression and the New Deal led the national government to take on a variety of new responsibilities. The New Deal extended the federal regulatory apparatus. By 1940, in a nation of 130 million people, the number of federal workers for the first time passed the 1 million mark. The Second World War brought federal civilian employment to 3.8 million in 1945. With peace, the federal establishment declined to around 2 million by 1950. Then growth resumed, reaching 2.8 million by the 1980s.

The New Deal years saw rising criticism of "big government" and "bureaucracy." Businessmen resented federal regulation. Conservatives worried about the impact of paternalistic government on individual self-reliance, on community responsibility, and on economic and personal freedom. The nation in effect renewed the old debate between Hamilton and Jefferson in the early republic, although with an ironic exchange of positions. For the Hamiltonian constituency, the "rich and well-born," once the advocate of affirmative government, now condemned government intervention, while the Jeffersonian constituency, the plain people, once the advocate of a weak central government and of states' rights, now favored government intervention.

In the 1980s, with the presidency of Ronald Reagan, the debate has burst out with unusual intensity. According to conservatives, government intervention abridges liberty, stifles enterprise, and is inefficient, wasteful, and arbitrary. It disturbs the harmony of the self-adjusting market and creates worse troubles than it solves. Get government off our backs, according to the popular cliché, and our problems will solve themselves. When government is necessary, let it be at the local level, close to the people. Above all, stop the inexorable growth of the federal government.

In fact, for all the talk about the "swollen" and "bloated" bureaucracy, the federal establishment has not been growing as inexorably as many Americans seem to believe. In 1949, it consisted of 2.1 million people. Thirty years later, while the country had grown by 70 million, the federal force had grown only by 750,000. Federal workers were a smaller percentage of the population in 1985 than they were in 1955—or in 1940. The federal establishment, in short, has not kept pace with population growth. Moreover, national defense and the postal service account for 60 percent of federal employment.

Why then the widespread idea about the remorseless growth of government? It is partly because in the 1960s the national government assumed new and intrusive functions: affirmative action in civil rights, environmental protection, safety and health in the workplace, community organization, legal aid to the poor. Although this enlargement of the federal regulatory role was accompanied by marked growth in the size of government on all levels, the expansion has taken place primarily in state and local government. Whereas the federal force increased by only 27 percent in the 30 years after 1950, the state and local government force increased by an astonishing 212 percent.

Despite the statistics, the conviction flourishes in some minds that the national government is a steadily growing behemoth swallowing up the liberties of the people. The foes of Washington prefer local government, feeling it is closer to the people and therefore allegedly more responsive to popular needs. Obviously there is a great deal to be said for settling local questions locally. But local government is characteristically the government of the locally powerful. Historically, the way the locally powerless have won their human and constitutional rights has often been through appeal to the national government. The national government has vindicated racial justice against local bigotry, defended the Bill of Rights against local vigilantism, and protected natural resources against local greed. It has civilized industry and secured the rights of labor organizations. Had the states' rights creed prevailed, there would perhaps still be slavery in the United States.

The national authority, far from diminishing the individual, has given most Americans more personal dignity and liberty than ever before. The individual freedoms destroyed by the increase in national authority have been in the main the freedom to deny black Americans their rights as citizens; the freedom to put small children to work in mills and immigrants in sweatshops; the freedom to pay starvation wages, require barbarous working hours, and permit squalid working conditions; the freedom to deceive in the sale of goods and securities; the freedom to pollute the environment—all freedoms that, one supposes, a civilized nation can readily do without.

"Statements are made," said President John F. Kennedy in 1963, "labelling the Federal Government an outsider, an intruder, an adversary. . . . The United States Government is not a stranger or not an enemy. It is the people of fifty states joining in a national effort. . . . Only a great national effort by a great people working together can explore the mysteries of space, harvest the products at the bottom of the ocean, and mobilize the human, natural, and material resources of our lands."

So an old debate continues. However, Americans are of two minds. When pollsters ask large, spacious questions—Do you think government has become too involved in your lives? Do you think government should stop regulating business?—a sizable majority opposes big government. But when asked specific questions about the practical work of government—Do you favor social security? unemployment compensation? Medicare? health and safety standards in factories? environmental protection? government guarantee of jobs for everyone seeking employment? price and wage controls when inflation threatens?—a sizable majority approves of intervention.

In general, Americans do not want less government. What they want is more efficient government. They want government to do a better job. For a time in the 1970s, with Vietnam and Watergate, Americans lost confidence in the national government. In 1964, more than three-quarters of those polled had thought the national government could be trusted to do right most of the time. By 1980 only one-quarter was prepared to offer such trust. But by 1984 trust in the federal government to manage national affairs had climbed back to 45 percent.

Bureaucracy is a term of abuse. But it is impossible to run any large organization, whether public or private, without a bureaucracy's division of labor and hierarchy of authority. And we live in a world of large organizations. Without bureaucracy modern society would collapse. The problem is not to abolish bureaucracy, but to make it flexible, efficient, and capable of innovation.

Two hundred years after the drafting of the Constitution, Americans still regard government with a mixture of reliance and mistrust—a good combination. Mistrust is the best way to keep government reliable. Informed criticism

12

is the means of correcting governmental inefficiency, incompetence, and arbitrariness; that is, of best enabling government to play its essential role. For without government, we cannot attain the goals of the Founding Fathers. Without an understanding of government, we cannot have the informed criticism that makes government do the job right. It is the duty of every American citizen to know our government—which is what this series is all about.

Service stations across America were affected by the gasoline shortage brought on by the 1973 Arab oil embargo. At the time of the crisis the United States imported almost half of its oil from Arab sources.

ONE

The Nation's Energy Agency

The winter of 1973–74 held many unpleasant surprises for Americans. The price of stock in oil companies was down on world financial markets. The costs of goods and services had risen, causing the dollar to lose purchasing power and interest rates to soar, a combination that contributed to the highest inflation rate in 20 years. An economy that had boomed since World War II showed signs of recession, as business activity slowed almost to a standstill. Many factors contributed to this situation, but most prominent among them was a full-fledged energy crisis.

Everyone from the president on down was shocked. No one had expected or foreseen the disaster. In 1966, a White House study had concluded that American energy supplies would last through the rest of the century and that energy prices would remain stable. As late as 1970, experts had predicted that the nation would have to import only 27 percent of its oil by 1980. Although by 1973 imports exceeded this amount, the government did little to change this potentially dangerous situation: Oil fueled the nation's factories, ran its transportation systems, and powered important components of its military. Any disruption in the supply of this vital energy resource threatened the country's national security and its entire economic foundation.

Yet until the 1970s, there had been no need for a single federal agency to coordinate the production and consumption of the nation's seemingly limitless supply of energy. Then, in October 1973, Arab oil producers cut off the supply of petroleum to the United States in retaliation for its support of Israel in the Yom Kippur War. In the months that followed, the price of oil more than tripled, and the cutback in supplies caused nationwide shortages.

The severity of the oil crisis alarmed the nation. Even after the embargo was lifted in the spring of 1974, the question of adequate energy supplies troubled many Americans. In 1977, newly elected president Jimmy Carter submitted a plan to Congress to consolidate a multitude of federal energy programs spread throughout the government under one Department of Energy (DOE). On August 4, 1977, Congress approved the Department of Energy Organization Act, and three months later the DOE officially began operations.

From the outset the DOE was heavily funded and massively staffed. Its large size frightened critics who saw in it the potential for abuse in the handling of energy concerns. They argued that because the DOE set oil and gas prices, it could potentially exert too much control over the nation's energy resources. Yet over the years most of the critics' fears have not materialized.

The Arab oil embargo forced the United States to accept that its oil, natural gas, and coal supplies are not limitless. After the severity of the embargo had passed, the DOE was able to turn its attention to conservation, nuclear energy, and alternative fuels. It has been working toward finding and developing other, nondepletable energy sources, most notably solar power. One promising source of solar energy is the photovoltaic cell, which can absorb sunlight and convert light energy directly into electricity. Department of Energy scientists are also studying ways of using geothermal energy (heat from the earth's interior) and ocean thermal energy (solar energy that is absorbed by the ocean) to produce electricity.

All of these energy sources are renewable and limitless. They are drawn from the climate and landscape of the United States, so the country will have no need to import them. Most of these renewable sources, as they are called, are still experimental and are as yet not widely used. But another alternative energy source—nuclear power—has been in use since World War II.

The energy released from the splitting of the atom—a process called fission—has not proven to be as safe or efficient as people had originally thought. In 1979, a breakdown in the water cooling system at the Three Mile Island nuclear power plant near Harrisburg, Pennsylvania, caused radioactive waste to be released into the atmosphere. Seven years later the Soviet Union's Chernobyl nuclear power plant caught fire and leaked nuclear waste, seriously

The Intercultural Center at Georgetown University in Washington, D.C., contains more than 4,400 photovoltaic modules, which convert sunlight directly into electricity for use in the university's power system. The DOE provided part of the funding for the project, which is the largest known roof-mounted photovoltaic system in the world.

endangering human, animal, and plant life. Department of Energy scientists are studying these accidents to better understand the weaknesses and dangers of nuclear energy and to develop improved technology for nuclear power plants. As a result of DOE recommendations, the federal government has modified its guidelines for nuclear reactors and has formulated new emergency plans for dealing with a nuclear disaster. Still, the public is not yet convinced that nuclear energy is safe.

Because the energy potential of nuclear power cannot be ignored, the DOE is studying the inverse of nuclear fission—nuclear fusion, whereby the nuclei of two or more atoms are joined together. Scientists believe that the energy derived from fusion will be safe, cheap, and inexhaustible. The DOE is an integral partner, along with universities and commercial companies, in the support of basic theoretical research in the study of energy and matter. It believes that fusion may prove to be the ultimate energy source.

The DOE is actively involved in other areas of nuclear energy that seriously affect both the security and well-being of the nation. The department oversees

A protester blocks the gate to the Three Mile Island nuclear power plant near Harrisburg, Pennsylvania, in May 1985. About 200 people gathered outside the plant to protest the use of nuclear power and the reopening of the damaged Unit 2 reactor.

the operation of various weapons plants that manufacture nuclear weapons and material for the U.S. military. It supervises the transportation of radioactive waste to repositories and provides interim storage facilities for this waste until it can be deposited at a permanent site. It also maintains armed security forces to protect DOE-operated nuclear facilities against sabotage, theft, or attack.

One of the most difficult problems the DOE has had to solve thus far has been encouraging the American public to think in terms of conserving energy. Methods of conservation include curtailing the wasteful use of automobiles and electricity, insulating homes, installing energy-efficient windows, and keeping thermostats at reasonable levels. The DOE is working toward these ends in the research it supports, funding such projects as the development of improved insulation materials and energy-saving appliances.

Despite all the hardships caused by the Arab oil embargo of 1973, some of the nation's leaders saw a positive side to the energy crisis. It erected an obstacle to the nation's progress that had to be addressed and that could not be

18

denied. As Secretary of the Interior Stewart Udall said in 1973, "I hope the Arabs don't turn the tap on, because the inevitable day when we must go through the wringer will be postponed." In other words, if the United States endured the hardship and faced the problem squarely, it would find solutions to the energy crisis. Otherwise, the country was in for a painful economic decline.

In April 1977, when President Jimmy Carter publicly unveiled his plan to create the Department of Energy, he said, "Our decision about energy will test the character of the American people and the ability of the President to govern the nation." In its short history the DOE, like the American people, has been tested and has survived. Its policies, though not always well received or universally accepted, affect not only the availability and type of fuel Americans use but also the progress the country makes toward reducing its dependence on foreign oil and strengthening its national security.

An offshore drilling rig in Mobile Bay, Alabama, operated by the Mobil Oil Company. Oil, the United States's primary energy source, provides almost half of the nation's energy.

TWO

The Joyride Is Over

It is difficult now to understand how so many people could have missed the warning signals of the 1973 Arab oil embargo. In hindsight, the evidence was there, but the government had not foreseen the possibility of an oil shortage. For many years the government had actually fostered the country's wasteful attitude toward energy.

In the 1930s, the nation's leaders encouraged the public to make maximum use of the nation's supplies of energy. Conservation of the country's valuable energy resources was never considered. In fact, the government kept oil and natural gas prices at such artificially low levels that Americans could hardly be criticized for wasting energy. After all, energy was cheap and seemed plentiful. Furthermore, these same low prices did not induce industry to explore alternative sources of energy, sources that would not run out.

The 1930s also saw the electrification of farms and homes outside the technologically advanced urban areas of America. With the creation of the federally run Tennessee Valley Authority (TVA) in 1933 and the Rural Electrification Administration (REA) in 1935, electricity was sent coursing through rural areas of the United States. Even though the TVA, which operated a series of dams along the Tennessee River, and a few other power companies produced electricity from hydroelectric plants, most of the country's ever-increasing demand for power was met by conventional, oil-fueled

21

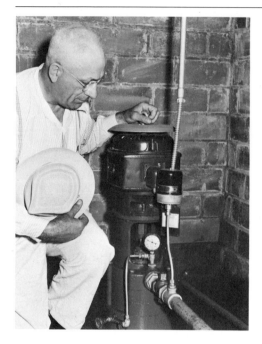

A Department of Agriculture agent inspects an electric water pump in Gundy County, Iowa, in 1939. Through the Rural Electrification Administration, which was created in 1935 to generate and distribute electricity to isolated rural areas of the United States, many jobs that had once been performed manually could now be executed by electrically powered machinery.

plants. (Hydroelectric energy is produced by water stored behind a dam. As water is released from the dam, it turns special water turbines that produce electricity.)

Ways of life and demographic patterns changed in the 1940s and 1950s. Veterans returning from World War II completed their education and bought houses with government assistance from the GI Bill. The nation prospered, and the size of the American family increased. People settled in and around cities, where the most jobs were located. Interstate highways now crisscrossed the country, and inexpensive gas provided an incentive for long family vacations by car. By 1970, 80 percent of all U.S. households owned at least one automobile and used it daily. Both men and women traveled to work and to play in "gas-guzzlers."

The United States, with less than one-tenth of the world's population, consumed one-third of the fuel used worldwide by the 1970s—and wasted an estimated 50 percent of that. Americans lacked an energy conscience because the oil supply seemed abundant and cheap. And until 1970 they always had another seemingly limitless source of energy to fall back on—coal. Coal was the most plentiful alternative energy source to oil. The Clean Air Act Amendments of 1970, however, set air-quality standards for pollutants

22

produced in the burning of coal. The utilities industry searched desperately for low-sulfur coal to meet the government restrictions, only to find it in the West, where federal law forbade them to strip-mine it from the surface of the earth. Utility companies had no choice but to continue to burn oil and natural gas to meet the public demand.

Americans never dreamed they would have to cut back their consumption of energy or even go without—never, that is, until the price of oil nearly quadrupled in 1973 as a result of the Arab oil embargo.

Playing Politics with Oil

On October 6, 1973, Syria and Egypt invaded Israel. The Israeli army quickly stopped the Syrians, but they could not squash the Egyptian offensive in the Sinai Desert. The Israelis turned to their most reliable ally, the United States,

An Israeli tank crew occupies a bomb-shattered street in Suez City, Egypt, in October 1973. United States support of Israel in the 1973 Yom Kippur War led Arab oil producers to cut off U.S. petroleum supplies, touching off a nationwide oil crisis.

for help. They wanted weapons, especially tanks, for use in the desert against the Egyptians, and they wanted the United States to supply them.

The oil-producing nations in the Middle East immediately recognized the threat American aid to Israel posed to their own national security. They also knew that America was vulnerable in one area that the Arabs could take advantage of—the United States's dependence on Arabian oil. A few months earlier, Libyan leader Colonel Muammar Qaddafi had effectively stymied the United States by simply refusing to supply the country with oil unless it became more receptive to Libyan needs. Qaddafi had shown the Arab countries just what power they could exert over their mighty Western opponent.

The powerful Arab American Oil Company (Aramco), which was headquartered in Saudi Arabia, was keenly aware of the real danger Qaddafi and his allies presented. Aramco's American partners, Texaco, Exxon, Mobil, and Standard Oil of California, knew that their Saudi Arabian partners would act against them if the United States aided Israel. The presidents of these companies sent a frantic memo to President Richard M. Nixon on October 12, 1973. They informed him that King Faisal of Saudi Arabia was considering cutting back oil production if the United States supplied weapons to Israel. Kuwait supported Faisal's plan, as did the other Arab oil-producing countries. Aramco bluntly told the president, "Much more than our commercial interests in the area is now at hazard. The real stakes are both our economy and our security."

Because of political pressures, President Nixon was obliged to aid the Israelis. By October 17th, the Israeli army was on the verge of defeating the Egyptians—with tanks and other munitions they had received from the Americans four days earlier. Saudi Arabia and the other Arab states retaliated, stopping oil shipments to the United States altogether and raising the price of oil by 70 percent. The United States was stunned, for it imported almost half of the oil that it used from Arabian sources.

When the winter of 1973 hit the country full force, even the most skeptical began to believe in the oil crisis. It was both domestic and international in scope, and the United States could not afford to ignore it. Everyone experienced the crisis firsthand. Public schools in the Midwest, where the winter that year was the most severe, were in session only three days a week. Airplanes leaving New York for the West Coast had to stop halfway to refuel because the airports from which they departed could not fill their tanks. Many factories went on half-day schedules. There was talk of skyrocketing heating bills, gasoline rationing, and even brownouts (cutbacks in electrical service).

Internationally, American diplomacy now had to take into account the impending Arab threat to the energy security of the United States—as well as of the whole Western world. Some people feared an American withdrawal of support for Israel. Everyone wondered how the richest and most technologically sophisticated nation in the world could be in such a position. Many Americans abruptly discovered what David Freeman, a science aide to President Carter, wryly observed: "The joyride is over."

The Federal Energy Administration

President Nixon had no single department to turn to and no united policy upon which to base his response to the Arab oil embargo. In October 1973, 64 different agencies were making energy decisions, agencies ranging from the Atomic Energy Commission to the Bureau of Mines to the Environmental Protection Agency. Nixon attacked the oil crisis on various fronts. In November 1973, he formulated a vague plan—called Project Independence— to wean the country from its dependence on foreign oil. It was not until January

President Richard M. Nixon meets with William E. Simon (left), the head of the Federal Energy Administration, in January 1974. Simon was faced with the difficult task of coordinating the nation's response to the fuel shortage caused by the 1973 Arab oil embargo.

25

1974, however, that Nixon put forth some concrete ideas for this program, which included accelerating nuclear power plant construction, increasing federal funding for energy-related research projects, and opening the seafloor off the continental shelf to oil and natural gas exploration.

In December 1973, Nixon had established the Federal Energy Office (FEO) to deal with the oil shortages caused by the Arab embargo. Five months later Congress replaced the FEO with the Federal Energy Administration (FEA). The FEA was to be headed by its own energy "czar." Nixon chose William E. Simon, who had directed the FEO, to lead the new agency. Simon's energy plan was a mixture of conservation incentives, such as restricting the retail sale of gasoline to individuals to 10 gallons apiece, and rigid adherence to the government's oil allocation guidelines. The guidelines, imposed in January 1974 in an effort to cut back on the nation's use of oil, required petroleum suppliers to provide gasoline retailers with the same percentage of oil that the retailer had sold in the same month of the previous year.

Nixon believed that the overuse of the automobile was one of the main sources of energy waste. In addition to the allocation guidelines, he attempted to force gasoline conservation by reducing the speed limit and by lowering emissions standards for automobiles. Consumer groups joined the conservation effort and called for more carpooling. No one, however, was ready to support outright gas rationing.

Energy Policy Under Ford and Carter

The FEA survived the political turmoil of the last years of the Nixon presidency and ultimately became the cornerstone of the Department of Energy. Meanwhile, oil prices had reached $11.56 a barrel—as opposed to a 1973 price of $4 a barrel—and analysts predicted they would go as high as $13. Nixon's successor, Gerald Ford, had little choice but to formulate an energy plan quickly. His blueprint was twofold. First, he would decontrol domestic-oil and natural-gas prices, which had been kept below world prices since 1970 in an effort to generate consumer demand and stimulate the sluggish economy. The decontrol of prices would enable domestic oil producers to obtain the market price for their petroleum, and the promise of higher revenues would encourage the exploration of new domestic reserves. Leasing offshore sites for drilling would further spur the development of domestic petroleum sources. Second, President Ford would ease restrictions on the burning of coal, loosen federal controls on strip-mining, promote conservation, and support the development

26

Coal from a strip mine in Asbury, Missouri, is shoveled directly from the earth's surface into a truck. Although this method of mining ruins the landscape, in the late 1970s the U.S. government eased federal restrictions on strip-mining to increase domestic supplies of fuel.

of nuclear power. He also advocated the creation of a single government agency devoted specifically to energy-related programs.

When Ford lost his election bid to Jimmy Carter in November 1976, his energy policy was replaced by that of the new president. For Carter, solving the energy crisis was a top priority, and the 95th Congress that convened in January 1977 reflected the urgency the nation felt. The *Congressional Quarterly* succinctly summed up the new government's philosophy. The 95th Congress, it reported, "had two agendas: energy and everything else."

Carter immediately pursued the idea of consolidating the energy-related programs of the federal government under one department. He felt that the creation of a superagency to unify and enforce energy policy had to be accomplished quickly if the United States wanted to protect its economic and national security. On March 1, 1977, he proposed a comprehensive energy program to Congress. Because of the diversity and scope of the program, the Speaker of the House, Thomas P. "Tip" O'Neill, appointed a special committee

President Jimmy Carter signs the Department of Energy Act on August 4, 1977. The act consolidated the energy-related programs of a multitude of agencies into one cabinet-level department.

to consider the proposal. Ohio congressman Lud Ashley chaired the committee, which drafted legislation for the program, ferried it through all the committees that needed to approve it, and presented it before the full House. Carter's energy plan met with less success in the Senate, however. The president's proposal became mired in five Senate committees. President Carter vigorously lobbied members of the Senate, but he was unable to win complete approval of his entire energy program.

Both the Senate and the House did, however, approve the most important item on Carter's energy agenda—the creation of the Department of Energy. On August 4, 1977, Congress passed the Department of Energy Organization Act, and the following day James R. Schlesinger was sworn in as the first secretary of energy. Schlesinger, an economist and former chairman of the Atomic Energy Commission, was faced with the monumental tasks of organizing the DOE and orchestrating the government's response to the energy crisis. President Carter drew a clear picture of what he wanted the new department to do: "Our most basic and difficult question is how to raise the price of scarce energy with minimum disruption of our economic system and greater equity in bearing the financial burden."

Oil Deregulation

Like his predecessor, Carter believed the answer to the nation's energy problems was in the decontrol of oil and natural gas prices. Many members of Congress also agreed. In October 1977, there were five separate energy bills in the Senate alone that touched on the issue of the decontrol of fuel prices. None of these bills, however, could overcome the partisan struggles between representatives of the oil- and gas-producing states (who wanted total decontrol of prices), the energy industry (which wanted the government to ease federal controls on the production and use of energy), and environmentalists and antinuclear-power groups (who called for stricter regulations governing the emission of pollution and the operation of nuclear power plants). Most members of Congress agreed that the basic problem underlying the energy crunch was that domestic oil prices—and to some extent natural gas prices—were too low.

America's allies in NATO (the North Atlantic Treaty Organization), an alliance of Western democracies formed after World War II to counterbalance the strength of the Soviet Union and its allies, also exerted pressure on President Carter to raise U.S. oil prices. Price-controlled oil contributed indirectly to rampant inflation throughout the Western world. Because the prices were low, the United States was wasting oil, and it was not exploring for new domestic wells or other sources of energy. The result was a nationwide oil shortage that hurt industry, causing workers to be laid off and the prices of manufactured goods to rise. The cost of many items increased, including those goods the rest of the world wanted to buy from the United States. Interest rates on loans to foreign governments and American consumers skyrocketed, as the combination of inflated prices and the decline in the value of the dollar forced U.S. banks to raise their interest rates.

President Carter, however, hesitated to decontrol oil prices without strictly monitoring their rise so that consumers would not fall victim to oil company greed. He wanted to gradually bring U.S. oil prices in line with prices in the rest of the world, and he set a target date of 1980 for total decontrol. He pushed for drastic consumer cutbacks as the best way to decrease demand and increase the fuel supply. His energy plan, which Congress approved on

October 15, 1978, clearly demonstrated this reasoning. The policy penalized automobile manufacturers for producing cars that consumed large amounts of gas. It ordered electric companies to promote energy conservation and to help consumers insulate their buildings by providing information on insulation and giving price breaks to people who installed insulation. It mandated that home appliances become energy efficient and established minimum efficiency requirements. It offered tax incentives to people who carpooled and used the alternate fuel gasohol, a blend of gasoline and alcohol that contains 10 percent ethyl alcohol (ethanol) and 90 percent unleaded gasoline.

The following year, 1979, was a critical one for U.S. energy policy, a year that solidified public and congressional opinion and strengthened President Carter's resolve. Three major events occurred that shaped the American perception of the energy problem and influenced its solutions. In January, an Islamic revolution toppled the shah of Iran and interrupted oil supplies to the United States. On March 28, an uncontrolled radioactive gas leak at the Three Mile Island nuclear power plant in Pennsylvania dimmed American hopes for a

The members of OPEC convene in Abu Dhabi, United Arab Emirates, in December 1978. One month later the group raised its oil prices by 50 percent, triggering the United States's second oil crisis of the decade.

nuclear solution to the oil and gas shortage. And between January and July, the Organization of Petroleum Exporting Countries (OPEC), a group of Third World oil-producing nations (including many Arab countries) that coordinates the oil policies of its members, raised the price of a barrel of oil 50 percent, sending the U.S. inflation rate even higher. Eight hundred thousand Americans lost their jobs as factories and businesses cut production when they were unable to meet the rising cost of energy. Lines of cars appeared at gas stations because of the tight rules that governed the allocation of petroleum. In protest, truck drivers went on strike, blockaded major roads, and even rioted in Levittown, Pennsylvania.

Once again, Americans were reminded of how dependent they were on imported oil. The international implications were obvious to all: skyrocketing inflation and unemployment worldwide, political instability in the Middle East, and worse yet, possible Soviet intervention in the Persian Gulf and total inaccessibility to vital Arab oil.

Almost everyone in the United States had a favorite villain to blame for the crisis. To some it was the oil companies, which seemed to be lining their pockets with huge fortunes at the public's expense. To others, the DOE and its gas-allocation rules were the real culprits. Many people could not afford to take a long automobile trip during the summer of 1979 because the price of gas was so high. They stayed home instead, which drained local supplies of gasoline. Gas pumps in cities and suburban areas dried up because, according to the allocation rules, service stations could not be resupplied once they consumed their quota for the month. Although the DOE was bitterly criticized for these regulations, Secretary Schlesinger had in fact tried to persuade Congress to abolish price controls and the Nixon allocation rules. Both he and President Carter, however, had a difficult task ahead of them in convincing the legislators on Capitol Hill to support Carter's energy proposals.

Carter's Comprehensive Energy Plan

In June 1979, President Carter met with the leaders of six other countries in Tokyo, Japan, to discuss solutions to the world energy crisis. He agreed at the talks to cut U.S. imports of oil by 1 million barrels a day. Although that amount was inconceivable to most critics, Carter gambled that certain results would follow the decontrol of oil and natural gas prices in the United States. First, higher oil prices would force industry to switch to natural gas. The resulting import reduction would also make exploration for new energy sources look more promising as a money-making enterprise. Furthermore, the president hoped his action would encourage some businesses to convert to or return to coal. If these things happened, then Carter felt the country could survive the cutback.

In July 1979, President Carter unveiled a comprehensive energy plan that centered on price decontrol, enforced conservation, and government-funded research. Domestic oil prices would be allowed to rise slowly over the next two years from $13 a barrel to a maximum of $26 a barrel. The incredible profits oil companies would accrue as a result of the deregulation of prices would be subject to a 50 percent "windfall profits" tax, a tax on oil production intended to partially counteract the excessive profits, or windfall, that oil producers were expected to reap through price decontrols. Carter reckoned that this tax would yield the federal government somewhere in the vicinity of $220 billion in the 1980s, at least half of which would be pumped back into the petroleum industry and earmarked for exploration and research. He ordered conservation of dwindling oil supplies by creating the Emergency Building Temperature Restrictions program, which stipulated the minimum and maximum temperatures for cooling and heating in public buildings.

Carter's energy program, though far reaching, was not without its critics. Almost everyone agreed that oil and natural gas had to be decontrolled. The most cynical theorized that higher prices would indeed result in lower consumption. But when the lesser demand created a slight oil glut, they argued, Americans would cease their conservation efforts and stop looking for alternative energy sources. Conservatives complained that the windfall profits tax should be rejected on the grounds that it was prejudiced against the petroleum industry. They pointed out that exploration would be easier and more profitable if the government and environmentalists would open up new areas for development, mainly Alaska. Finally, if the oil companies were mistreated, the only result would be a drying up of domestic oil production and even more dependence on imported oil.

President Carter began an intensive effort to push his energy plan through Congress. His first move was to accept the resignation of Secretary Schlesinger. Schlesinger had become extremely unpopular with Congress and had taken the blame for the government's inability to solve the country's energy problems. Many people felt that he failed to fulfill the demands of his position. Environmentalists disapproved of his support of the nuclear power industry, which they saw as too dangerous to the environment and human life. Consumer groups opposed his efforts to decontrol oil and natural gas prices because the skyrocketing prices that would occur as a result of deregulation would hurt the

Workmen install a solar hot water heating system on the roof of the West Wing of the White House during Jimmy Carter's term as president. Carter persistently worked to decrease the nation's dependence on oil, and his energy policy may be one of the most enduring legacies of his administration.

average American. Conservatives feared he had too much power and could, if he wanted, control the nation's energy supplies through the government's stringent gas-allocation policy.

In July 1979, Schlesinger was succeeded by a far less controversial man, Charles William Duncan, Jr., formerly the president of the Coca-Cola Company. Prior to his appointment as secretary of energy, Duncan had been President Carter's deputy secretary of defense and was highly regarded for his management skills.

Although the appointment of Duncan as secretary was a politically popular move, Congress nevertheless altered Carter's energy plan. It imposed a windfall profits tax on petroleum but mandated a rate ranging from 30 percent to 70 percent, based on different categories of oil, rather than the straight 50 percent Carter had proposed. It removed restrictions on how the tax revenues could be spent. The tax would remain in effect until October 1993, unless $227 billion had been collected before that date. In July 1980, Congress approved the

The Trans-Alaska Pipeline, an 800-mile oil pipeline connecting Prudhoe Bay to Valdez, Alaska, transports oil from the Alaskan North Slopes, which contain the largest oil fields in the United States. Until 1980, federal environmental laws greatly restricted oil exploration in the interior and offshore regions of Alaska.

Energy Security Act. This bill created the Synthetic Fuels Corporation, a public corporation, to make loans to companies interested in developing synthetic fuels from sources such as shale rock and tar sands (sands that contain a sticky substance known as bitumen, which can be refined into fuel). Finally, on December 2, 1980, Congress passed the Alaska National Interest Lands Conservation Act, which allowed 100 percent of Alaska's offshore areas and 95 percent of its interior to be explored for oil and gas.

The Reagan Years

Almost all of President Carter's energy plan had been installed by the time he left the White House in 1981, and it may be one of the most enduring legacies of his tenure as president. Carter's successor, Ronald Reagan, sought to relieve overtaxed Americans and a government drowning in bureaucratic red tape. There was speculation that the new president would reduce the size of the DOE, if not abolish it entirely. Reagan thought that the solution to America's energy problems lay in the removal of federal constraints in the production of energy and the promotion of competition among energy producers. His first secretary of energy, James B. Edwards, was a former governor of South Carolina and dentist by profession. Edwards, an ardent supporter of Reagan's political ideology, summed up the administration's energy agenda in one sentence: "Just move some of the regulations out of the way and get rid of some of the restraints and you can solve all of our problems energy-wise in a short period of time, say four to six years." At one point Edwards suggested dismantling the DOE so that its biggest programs, weapons and energy research and nuclear energy, could be turned over to the private sector, where he believed market forces would resolve the nation's energy problems. Both Reagan and Edwards strongly believed that if the energy industry were deregulated and the free market forces of supply and demand were allowed to operate unencumbered, the twin problems of supply and consumption would be solved.

To this end, Reagan accelerated Carter's program of price deregulation, completely abolishing price controls on oil in 1981 and partially deregulating controls on natural gas in 1986. In 1987, he repealed the Fuel Use Act. He reduced both the Tennessee Valley Authority's and the Rural Electrification Administration's access to low-interest loans. Finally, he cut money for synthetic fuel research and eased restrictions on the energy standards set for home appliances.

President Ronald Reagan signs legislation repealing the 1978 Fuel Use Act as Secretary of Energy John S. Herrington (left) and Secretary of the Interior Donald P. Hodel look on. The act, which limited the use of natural gas and oil in some industrial facilities, was rescinded in May 1987.

Nevertheless, President Reagan could not dismantle the Department of Energy. It has a mission to pursue and a driving motivation—to prevent another decade like the 1970s, with its monumental energy problem and the resulting economic and social disruptions, from ever happening again.

The State of U.S. Energy Today

The DOE is as large and as multifaceted as its critics feared it would be. In 1977, the economist Milton Friedman worried that the DOE would "control the lifeblood of our economic system. . . But can our system survive Federal control of the pricing, the production, the distribution, [and] the import of energy?"

Yet the nation's supplies of energy are more secure today than they were in 1977. At the same time the country is less dependent than it was on Arabian oil. Although these advances cannot be underestimated, the DOE is acutely aware that the United States has far from solved its energy problem. Recognizing that reserves of oil and natural gas are nearing depletion, the department has begun to search for ways to conserve the nation's energy supplies and further lessen its dependence on foreign imports. It is actively pursuing research into alternative energy sources and is attempting to make nuclear power both safe and affordable.

A worker at a storage site in Idaho checks barrels containing low-level nuclear waste for radiation leakage. The DOE's Office of Civilian Radioactive Waste Management supports programs that contribute to the construction of permanent repositories for nuclear waste and manages interim facilities to store this waste until it can be deposited in a permanent repository.

THREE

The Creation of
a Superagency

On October 1, 1977, the DOE formally began operations as the 12th cabinet-level department. From the outset it was a massive superagency. Its initial budget, an astronomical $10.5 million, was in part derived from its predecessors: the Energy Research and Development Administration, the Federal Energy Administration, the Federal Power Commission, and the energy-related programs of several other federal agencies.

The Energy Research and Development Administration (ERDA), along with the Nuclear Regulatory Commission (NRC), had replaced the Atomic Energy Commission (AEC) in 1974. The Energy Research and Development Administration had inherited those AEC programs having to do with the research and development of atomic energy—including the development of nuclear weapons. (The NRC had taken over the licensing and inspection of nuclear power plants.) At the same time, the research programs of various agencies linked to the production of energy came under the control of ERDA. These included the Bureau of Mines's projects in fossil-fuel technology, the National Science Foundation's experiments in solar and geothermal energy, and the Environmental Protection Agency's research in alternative automobile technology. When the DOE absorbed ERDA in 1977, it assumed all these tasks.

Secretary of Energy James R. Schlesinger unveils the Department of Energy plaque on October 1, 1977, the DOE's first official day of operation. The DOE was temporarily headquartered at 776 Jackson Place in Washington, D.C., until it moved to its present location at 1000 Independence Avenue S.W. in May 1978.

The DOE also took over those programs previously administered by the Federal Energy Administration (FEA). The FEA was created in 1974 to address the problems caused by the Arab oil embargo and to carry out the government's policies pertaining to the price regulation and allocation of domestic oil. In conjunction with these duties, the FEA directed the federal effort to encourage the conservation of energy and the promotion of coal as an alternative energy source to oil or natural gas. The FEA was also responsible for maintaining the Strategic Petroleum Reserve, a reservoir of government-owned oil stockpiled in case of disruptions in the supply of foreign oil. In addition, it operated the National Energy Information Center, which gathered and analyzed statistics and other information about energy.

When Congress passed the Department of Energy Organization Act in August 1977, it altered various aspects of the agency that President Carter had originally proposed. It opposed Carter's plan to place the Federal Power Commission (FPC), which regulated the price of electricity and natural gas and the licensing of hydroelectric power plants, under the direct control of the secretary of energy. The members of Congress did not want to give one person too much power in determining the cost of the nation's major energy sources. Therefore, Congress created the Federal Energy Regulatory Commission (FERC) to administer most of the programs formerly carried out by the FPC. The Federal Energy Regulatory Commission, though a part of the DOE, is an independent agency and does not report directly to the secretary of energy.

Among the energy-related programs that the DOE inherited from the Department of the Interior was the oversight of five federal agencies that generate and sell hydroelectric power: the Southeastern Power Administration, which provides electricity to states in the southeastern United States; the Southwestern Power Administration, which serves Arkansas, Kansas, Louisiana, Missouri, Oklahoma, and Texas; the Bonneville Power Administration, which serves the Pacific Northwest; the Alaska Power Administration, which

The federally owned Hungry Horse Dam in Montana generates hydroelectric power for the DOE's Bonneville Power Administration (BPA). The BPA sells the electricity produced by its network of dams to residential and business customers in the Pacific Northwest and provides nearly half of the power used there.

not only sells hydroelectric power but also conducts research into new sources of energy; and the Western Area Power Administration, which supplies power to 15 central and western states. The proceeds from the sale of power are used to offset operating and maintenance costs and to repay the government's investment in the projects.

Finally, the DOE took over several small, energy-related programs previously directed by the Department of Housing and Urban Development, the Department of Commerce, the Department of the Navy, and the Interstate Commerce Commission, as well as the management of the Naval Petroleum Reserves and the Naval Oil Shale Reserves. Formerly maintained by the Defense Department, these reservoirs of liquid fuel were established in the early 20th century to provide emergency supplies for national defense in the event of war.

The Secretary of Energy

The DOE is headed by a secretary who is appointed by the president and confirmed by the Senate. The secretary advises the president on energy matters and acts as a public spokesperson for the policies of the federal government. He or she is the liaison between the DOE and other federal agencies and heads the Energy Coordinating Committee, a panel made up of the secretaries of state, treasury, defense, and other federal officials that coordinates U.S. energy policy and management.

As a member of the president's cabinet, the secretary of energy is one of the most influential people in the country and holds enormous sway over federal energy policy. He or she carries out the overall, long-range planning for the DOE and formulates its policy. With the aid of a deputy secretary, the secretary directs and supervises the department's administration and oversees its activities.

Organizational Structure

An extensive network of people assists the secretary of energy in carrying out the programs and policies of the DOE. Next in command after the secretary is the deputy secretary, who participates in the planning, direction, and control of the department. Should the secretary be unable to perform his or her duties for any reason, the deputy secretary takes over in the interim.

The under secretary of the DOE is its chief operating officer. He or she manages the various departments and agencies within the DOE and oversees programs involving research and development. The under secretary also supervises projects involving energy conservation and renewable energy technology and promotes increased energy efficiency by industry and the general public.

The general counsel serves as the DOE's chief legal adviser and is responsible for the acquisition of patents on inventions created by DOE scientists, the legal aspects of proposed legislation, and the handling of all litigation on behalf of the DOE. The general counsel does not, however, investigate cases of fraud or abuse or audit various agencies within the DOE. These jobs are performed by the DOE's inspector general.

Fifteen offices or programs, each headed by a director or assistant secretary, and two administrations are headquartered at the DOE in Washington, D.C. In addition, the department oversees the operation of various field offices and hydroelectric power projects located throughout the United States.

The Office of Policy, Planning, and Analysis advises the secretary of energy on the formulation, analysis, and evaluation of national energy policy. It helps the various assistant secretaries identify major energy issues and analyze information relevant to the department's programs. It continually monitors the status of the nation's energy resources and uses this information to draft

The DOE's headquarters in Washington, D.C. The department also maintains field offices and hydroelectric power projects throughout the United States.

43

legislation and prepare the National Energy Policy Plan, a blueprint of the energy policy that the president submits to Congress every two years.

The administrative services of the DOE, including personnel and finance, are carried out by the Office of Management and Administration. This office ensures that the DOE complies with equal employment opportunity laws in the hiring of personnel and handles issues pertaining to civil rights. It manages DOE property and administers the department's program for the award of contracts to commercial companies that provide goods to or perform services for the DOE.

The Office of Hearings and Appeals hears and resolves the cases of individuals and organizations seeking exemption from the DOE's rules and regulations. The Board of Contract Appeals, on the other hand, decides on contract-related issues raised by outside contractors who perform services for the DOE or operate government-owned facilities.

The Congressional, Intergovernmental, and Public Affairs division of the DOE is the principal point of contact between the DOE and federal, state, and local governments and the general public. It also serves as the liaison between the DOE and Congress, coordinating the appearances of DOE officials at congressional hearings, tracking legislation relevant to the department, and informing Congress of all DOE activities. The assistant secretary for congressional, intergovernmental, and public affairs is an advocate for consumers and actively promotes competition within the energy industry so that the public will benefit from improved service and lower prices.

Two offices within the DOE, the Office of Minority Economic Impact and the Office of Small and Disadvantaged Business Utilization, are concerned with how energy issues and DOE policies affect minority groups and the disadvantaged. The Office of Minority Economic Impact reports on ways that minorities—including minority businesses and educational institutions—can participate in the energy programs of the DOE. It provides loans to minority-owned businesses to assist in the preparation of bids or proposals for DOE contracts. The Office of Small and Disadvantaged Business Utilization is responsible for ensuring that a portion of the department's contracts with outside contractors are awarded to small and disadvantaged businesses, such as those owned by women.

Because all energy production and research have profound immediate and long-term effects on the environment and on public health and safety, the DOE maintains an Office of Environment, Safety, and Health to ensure that its programs comply with environmental safety and health regulations. The office also acts as a liaison between the DOE and other federal agencies, such as the

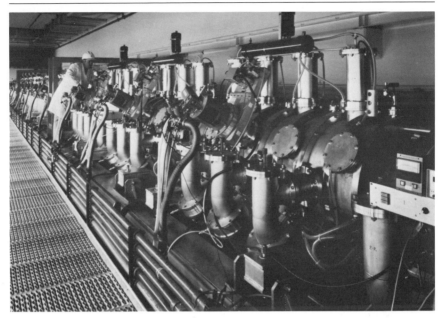

The flash X-ray facility at Lawrence Livermore National Laboratory in Livermore, California. The laboratory, which conducts research for the DOE, is operated by the University of California.

Environmental Protection Agency, to keep informed of any regulatory measures and specific actions on their part that may affect DOE operations.

During the 1980s the DOE spent more and more of its time and resources on researching and developing new sources of energy. One of the most heavily funded divisions within the DOE is the Office of Energy Research, which conducts basic research in the areas of engineering, chemistry, mathematical and computer sciences, geosciences, and botanical and microbiological sciences. In most cases this research is carried out at government laboratories located throughout the country and at hundreds of universities nationwide. The Advanced Energy Projects subprogram attempts to apply some of the energy-related concepts arrived at through basic research to actual situations. It directs the DOE's programs in high-energy physics, which involve the study of matter and energy. The Office of Energy Research also investigates the environmental and human safety aspects of its research and keeps track of international scientific advances.

Three programs within the DOE are devoted to the study of specific types of energy: fossil energy, renewable energy, and nuclear energy. The Office of

The Nevada desert is pockmarked with indentations such as this 1,200-foot-wide crater, the visible remains of an underground nuclear weapons test conducted in July 1962. Since 1951, the DOE and its predecessor agencies have tested nuclear weapons at the Nevada Test Site near Las Vegas.

Fossil Energy conducts research involving the exploration and production of petroleum, coal, and natural gas. It concentrates on the long-term and often expensive development of general technology and knowledge in the hopes that private industry will then further develop, and ultimately market, an advanced form of this technology. The office maintains two energy technology centers and a variety of other field laboratories to help commercial enterprises discover ways of maximizing the shrinking reserves of fossil fuels. It manages the government's Strategic Petroleum Reserve and Naval Petroleum and Oil Shale Reserves.

The Office of Conservation and Renewable Energy directs those DOE programs concerning nondepletable energy sources, such as the sun, wind, and water. Unlike fossil fuels, these sources of energy are limitless and are constantly renewed. The office oversees research and development programs designed to increase the output and use of renewable energy and improve energy efficiency around the home and in the workplace. It promotes conservation by offering financial assistance to states wishing to weatherproof

46

the homes of low-income families and to schools, hospitals, and nonprofit organizations that want to implement conservation measures.

The Office of Nuclear Energy is one of the most important divisions of the DOE. It carries out the department's research and development programs that pertain to atomic energy. The scope of its activities ranges from the development of advanced nuclear reactor systems for both civilian and governmental use to the creation and application of new space and weapon technologies to the discovery of improved methods for producing nuclear fuel. The office is responsible for overseeing the decontamination of government-owned—and in some cases privately owned—sites exposed to radioactive wastes. It is studying the core reactor of the damaged nuclear power plant at Three Mile Island in an effort to better understand the effects and risks of nuclear energy.

Tied to the DOE's Office of Nuclear Energy is its Office of Defense Programs. Both divisions conduct nuclear weapons research, but the Office of Defense Programs is primarily involved with the production, testing, and retirement of the nation's nuclear weapons and the disposal of defense-related nuclear waste. It is also responsible for the production of all nuclear materials used in the weapons program, including the enrichment of uranium, whereby uranium is converted into nuclear fuel. The Office of Defense Programs carries out intelligence-gathering activities in areas that pertain to national security and energy supplies. It conducts research related to the Strategic Defense Initiative, or "Star Wars" technology, a theoretical weapons system that may be able to destroy an incoming nuclear attack in space, and verifies adherence to international arms control agreements.

The Office of Civilian Radioactive Waste Management, created under the Nuclear Waste Policy Act of 1982, supports programs that contribute to the construction of permanent repositories for nuclear waste. It also manages interim facilities that store nuclear waste until it can be deposited in a permanent repository. In addition, it supervises the transportation of radioactive waste to the repositories and conducts research in storage technology. The costs of maintaining these programs are paid for by the private companies that generate the radioactive waste and are administered by the DOE through the Nuclear Waste Fund.

The search for and development of energy resources can have international repercussions. For this reason the DOE maintains an Office of International Affairs and Energy Emergencies to assess the policies of foreign countries that directly affect the United States either environmentally, legally, or by treaty. It also ensures that federal international energy policies and programs are in line with the goals, legislation, and treaty obligations of the U.S. government. The office cooperates with other nations in their quest for sources of energy and monitors the fluctuation of world energy prices. It prepares contingency plans for emergency situations, such as the nuclear accident that occurred at Chernobyl in April 1986, and tests and evaluates these response plans.

Two administrations, the Energy Information Administration (EIA) and the Economic Regulatory Administration (ERA), are headquartered at the DOE building in Washington. The EIA is the nation's primary source of energy information. Its administrator directs the collection, analysis, evaluation, and distribution of economic and statistical information on energy resources, reserves, production, consumption, distribution, and technology. The EIA staffs the DOE's public reading room and maintains a telephone line to provide energy information to private citizens, libraries, industry, the news media, foreign governments, and others.

The ERA administers the DOE's regulatory programs. It ensures that energy producers adhere to the government's guidelines on the import and export of natural gas and electricity. Until 1981, when price and allocation controls on oil were lifted, the ERA was responsible for enforcing the federal regulations that governed the petroleum industry. It audits petroleum firms and prosecutes companies found to have overcharged the public on the price of petroleum.

The Federal Energy Regulatory Commission (FERC) is an independent agency within the DOE and does not report directly to the secretary of energy. It is responsible for administering most of the government's energy-related regulatory programs. Its five-member commission establishes rates and charges for the transportation and sale of natural gas and for the transmission and sale of electricity. It also sets rates for the transportation of oil by pipeline and licenses hydroelectric power plants.

Much of the DOE's research in energy production is performed by private contractors who use government-owned facilities run by the DOE. The department maintains eight operations offices to serve as a link between the contractors and their laboratories and DOE headquarters. These offices are located in Albuquerque, New Mexico; Argonne, Illinois; Idaho Falls, Idaho; Las Vegas, Nevada; Oak Ridge, Tennessee; Richland, Washington; Oakland, California; and Aiken, South Carolina. The DOE also maintains special offices that oversee the management of the Strategic Petroleum Reserve, the Naval Petroleum and Oil Shale Reserves, and the development of nuclear reactors for the U.S. Navy's nuclear submarines.

A dry cask used for storing high-level spent, or used, nuclear fuel. The DOE conducted extensive tests on the design and safety of such casks, which are stored aboveground on concrete pads.

Directing the Nation's Energy Supply

The DOE is just as crucial today as it was in 1977. Long-term, high-risk technological research in energy-related fields would hardly be possible without its sponsorship. Conservation programs, the sale of power—even nuclear weapons production—all take direction from the DOE. The department has become a clearinghouse for the collection and analysis of energy data on a nationwide, and worldwide, level.

In the 1970s the DOE played the role of the energy regulator. In the 1980s it began to search for answers to the energy crunch, not just for ways of surviving from one energy crisis to the next. The answers it uncovers will ultimately provide the energy that fuels the nation in the 1990s and beyond. As President Reagan stated on the 10th anniversary of the creation of the DOE in 1987, "By combining the technology of today with the promise and vision of American know-how tomorrow, America will continue to be in the forefront of energy production into the 21st century."

49

*At this DOE-funded project in Osage County, Oklahoma, the Phillips Petro-
leum Company is perfecting a method of enhancing the recovery of residual
oil from depleted wells. The DOE works with members of the oil and natural
gas industries to maximize the amount of fossil fuels extracted from the earth.*

FOUR

The Problem
with Fossils

The United States obtains 90 percent of its fuel from oil, natural gas, and coal. All three of these substances were formed millions of years ago from the fossilized remains of prehistoric plants and animals. These fossil fuels, once considered to be limitless and abundant, are, in fact, nonrenewable. Once they are used up, they cannot be replaced.

As the nation's energy agency, the DOE is charged with finding ways to address the diminishing supply of fossil fuels. Enhanced domestic oil production through the increased drilling of wells, the withdrawal of any remaining oil and natural gas from old wells, and the substitution of coal are the backbone of the DOE's fossil-fuel policy. The department is coupling a conservation drive aimed at homes, businesses, and transportation with a stockpiling of oil in the Strategic Petroleum Reserve to avert a future fossil-fuel crisis. Finally, the DOE is an active participant in international forums on energy technology, oil sharing, and environmental problems.

The unanswered questions about fossil fuels are: How much is left? And when will it run out? Fossil-fuel supplies are measured in various ways. "Resources" are the total supply of fuel available, whether they are as yet untapped or currently being produced. "Estimated reserves" are fossil-fuel sources that experts believe must exist but are yet to be discovered. "Reserves" are

51

pockets of fuel that are still in the ground. The most meaningful measurement to the consumer, however, is "productive capacity," or the amount of fossil fuel that can actually be delivered to consumers on a daily basis.

The productive capacity of the United States is an indicator of the drain the country puts on its energy resources. The nation used 19 million barrels of oil per day in 1978. By 1988, it had managed to trim almost 2 million barrels daily from the 1978 figure, but the cutback is still not enough.

The United States obtains a significant percentage of its oil from foreign producers, its largest suppliers being Canada, Mexico, and Venezuela. Although the country reduced its oil imports from 47 to 35 percent between 1977 and 1987, the marked decline in oil prices in 1986 led many people to abandon their efforts to conserve energy. As a result, oil imports have again begun to rise.

The best alternative to importing oil is to make better use of America's own energy resources. Until recently, however, there was little incentive for domestic energy producers to develop U.S. supplies. Between 1978 and 1979, for example, oil companies drilled 1,819 wells in 19 states with estimated

The world's tallest offshore oil platform is towed to its destination in the Gulf of Mexico in May 1988. When erected it will be taller than the world's tallest building, the Sears Tower in Chicago. The decline of oil prices in 1986 led many people to abandon their efforts to conserve energy, and oil consumption has again begun to rise.

reserves of 2 billion gallons. The same companies drilled only 28 wells in Alaska, which has estimated reserves of 76 billion gallons. The reason that oil companies did not pursue domestic sources more diligently is easy to discover. First, companies that drilled and found nothing were able to claim huge losses and thereby obtain enormous tax breaks. Second, strict environmental restrictions and leasing policies made exploration in Alaska almost impossible. Third, President Carter's energy program authorized the funding of research in synthetic fuels, liquid or gaseous fuels produced from resources such as shale, tar sands, and coal. The oil or gas derived from these sources is synthetic or man-made in that it does not occur naturally in these substances—as do petroleum and natural gas—and must be converted to a liquid or gaseous state through engineering processes. The promise of synthetic fuels attracted the attention of some oil companies, which cut exploration for fossil fuels and instead became involved in synthetic fuel development. Finally, federal controls on the price of oil and natural gas made the high cost of drilling new wells financially impractical.

With the opening of Alaska's lands for oil and gas exploration and the removal of price controls on gasoline in the early 1980s, oil producers now have more incentive to develop new domestic resources. The DOE is working with members of the oil and natural gas industry to maximize the amount of fuel taken from the ground. Along with several private corporations it is investigating ways of recovering oil from depleted reservoirs by applying microorganisms and chemicals to the rock surface surrounding aging wells. This technique enhances the recovery of oil that cannot be removed through conventional drilling methods. In conjunction with natural gas companies, the DOE is perfecting a drill that will cut horizontally through deep shale to release previously inaccessible pockets of gas.

Cleaning Up Coal

Perhaps the most promising form of fossil-fuel energy is coal. It is estimated that the nation's coal reserves will last 700 years. This huge supply is not fully utilized because the government has placed stringent regulations on how coal may be mined and burned. The strip mines necessary for securing coal ruin the landscape, and the miners themselves are subjected to hazardous situations. Some 200 miners die each year in mine accidents, and long-term mine-related illnesses, such as black lung, a respiratory disease, cost the government $1 billion each year in disability payments.

The burning of high-sulfur coal results in tremendous pollution and is believed to be a cause of acid rain. Acid rain is formed when sulfur and nitrogen are released into the atmosphere and are trapped in clouds, returning to the earth as highly acidic rain, hail, or snow. Acid rain can adversely affect plant and animal life, pollute drinking water, and harm crops and soil.

The DOE, through its Clean Coal Technology Demonstration Program, is spearheading the rehabilitation of coal as a major U.S. energy source. It has selected seven companies to develop projects that employ new, innovative coal technologies. These model projects will then be used to demonstrate that coal can be burned without detriment to the environment, and the new technology will ultimately be marketed commercially. Another DOE research program is studying how to remove sulfur dioxide and nitrogen oxide, the lethal components in acid rain, from burned coal.

The problem of sulfur emission can be bypassed by converting coal to methane gas, which can then be used to produce electricity. About one-third of the coal's energy is lost in the process, however, and the conversion procedure, known as coal gasification, is expensive. The DOE, in conjunction with outside contractors, is working to develop gasification techniques that will be both energy efficient and economical. This technology, though still in its infancy, may be the most successful means of resolving the problem of pollutants emitted in the use of coal.

Conservation

The DOE's drive to curb the nation's demand for energy through effective and affordable conservation techniques has achieved some success. Ironically, much of the money the DOE uses to pay for conservation research and implementation has come from an unlikely source—the oil companies themselves. When the price of oil was decontrolled, the American consumer paid dearly: Between 1975 and 1980, heating-oil costs jumped 271 percent. Domestic oil companies, which sold their stockpiled reserves at the soaring market prices, made extremely large profits. In 1977, Congress asked the DOE to investigate charges that the oil companies were overpricing the cost of their oil. It also instructed the department to address the oil producers' complaints about the number and complexity of the regulations they were required by law to follow.

The DOE discovered that oil companies were overcharging the public. Its Economic Regulatory Administration audited some 20,000 oil companies and

Secretary of Energy John S. Herrington acknowledges receipt of a $2.1 billion check from the Exxon Corporation, which was found guilty of overcharging the public on the price of oil in 1978. The DOE audited some 20,000 oil companies for pricing violations and discovered that nearly 1,000 companies had overcharged the public by more than $8 billion.

discovered more than $8 billion in overcharges. The largest single fine collected—$2.1 billion—was from the Exxon Corporation in 1978. By 1987, the DOE had collected $6.1 billion of the overcharges, more than $4.8 billion of which was channeled into energy-related research and conservation efforts benefiting the public. These monies were disbursed to the states for use in local projects, such as weatherizing the homes of the elderly and handicapped and assisting low-income families with heating and cooling costs.

Conservation in the private and commercial sectors is a high priority with the DOE. The department funds both basic research aimed at advancing theoretical knowledge of nonfossil energy sources and applied research that actually tests these new concepts. Between 1977 and 1986 the DOE received 23,000 applications for financial assistance to support the development of energy-related inventions. It accepted 355 of these applications and awarded $19.2

million to help the 244 inventors involved continue their research. As of 1986, 36 of the DOE-supported inventions had been commercially marketed.

The DOE collects and publishes information on energy conservation and distributes this material free of charge on request. It facilitates the transfer of technology from the public to private industry and vice versa and makes sure that the many government-owned and government-run facilities in this country follow the department's guidelines for making efficient use of energy. It also issues voluntary guidelines to private industry for improving energy efficiency.

Energy Conservation Technology

To optimize the effect the DOE's conservation program has on energy consumers, the department has targeted specific users for special attention. Thirty-seven percent of the nation's energy is consumed by heavy industry, such as factories that manufacture steel or process foods. Another 36 percent is purchased by residential or commercial consumers, and the remaining 27 percent fuels the country's transportation system.

Because more than a third of the nation's energy is used to provide electricity and heat to homes and businesses, the DOE is actively involved in making public and private buildings energy efficient. Its work in this area includes efforts to develop improved materials for walls, roofs, and windows that will keep structures warm during the winter and cool during the summer. It is also studying the problems of ventilation and indoor air quality. The DOE encourages building contractors and the owners of old buildings to follow its energy guidelines, which recommend installing the most efficient insulation and using construction materials that have the highest efficiency ratings.

The DOE's Oak Ridge National Laboratory in Oak Ridge, Tennessee, has devised a method of evaluating the quality of insulation. An instrument measures the flow of heat into and out of buildings and assesses the insulation's efficiency. The Roof Research Center at the laboratory tests differing roof designs in a specially designed chamber that simulates various climatic conditions.

Windows that allow heat to escape on cold days and do not block the sun on hot days are a major source of energy waste. The DOE is working to develop a type of glass with low emissivity—that is, a glass that will reduce the transfer of heat from a warm environment to a cooler one. Scientists are on the verge of making a double-glazed window with as much insulation quality as a triple-glazed window. This breakthrough would eradicate the need to install storm windows over double-glazed windows, which is what most homeowners now do to provide added insulation during the winter.

Recent advances in the insulation of buildings have been so effective that a new problem has arisen: Airtight walls, windows, and roofs do not allow fresh air to flow in or out, which endangers the air quality in the building. With increasing frequency, homes and offices are testing positive for radon, a natural gas produced in the earth. When concentrated in a building, radon pollution can increase the risk of developing cancer. The DOE has constructed a system to measure the amount of radon in indoor air. It is studying the effects of diminished air circulation and is experimenting with alternative energy systems, such as air pumps, that could promote the exchange of indoor and outdoor air.

Through its Office of Buildings and Community Systems the DOE sets energy standards for the construction of new buildings. Although these

The DOE's Mobile Window Thermal Test (MoWiTT) facility measures the energy efficiency of windows and skylights under various outdoor climate conditions and simulated interior conditions. The DOE publishes technological information on the design and construction of buildings and distributes this information to individuals and organizations in the private sector for use in increasing energy efficiency.

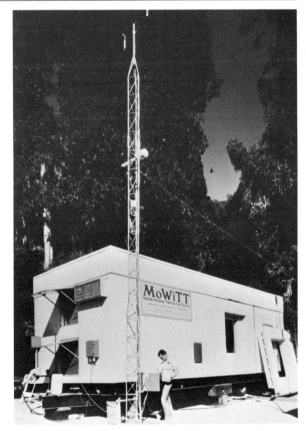

regulations are purely voluntary for commercial and residential structures, U.S. government buildings must meet DOE standards. The Office of Buildings and Community Systems collects and assesses data and publishes technological information on the design, construction, and updating of both recent and old buildings. This information is distributed to individuals and organizations in the private sector for use in increasing energy efficiency.

In 1985, the DOE created the Manchester Project, a scale model that demonstrated how old, abandoned, and substandard housing in an inner-city environment could be revitalized and made energy efficient. The project, which won the DOE a research prize from *Progressive Architecture* magazine, symbolizes the agency's commitment to extending the benefits of conservation throughout all social and economic levels of American society.

The largest consumer of the nation's energy supplies is heavy industry. Huge amounts of energy are lost in the manufacturing process. The DOE is looking into ways of saving this energy and using it more effectively, perhaps by producing energy from heat loss itself. It makes new technology—such as sophisticated heat exchangers and heat pumps, which produce electricity from the heat that is given off in the manufacturing process—available to commercial

The DOE is experimenting with electrically powered automobiles, such as this modified American Motors Pacer. The car, which is powered by 20 batteries, can reach a maximum speed of 56 MPH.

companies. The DOE also evaluates the technology of small firms and advises them on ways that they can improve their energy efficiency. Finally, it stresses conservation as a means of increasing profits.

The use of cars, planes, and other modes of transportation that depend on fossil fuels for power is a constant drain on the nation's energy supplies. The DOE is heavily involved in the research and development of alternative forms of transportation. Substitutes for the internal combustion engine, which is the type of engine used in nearly all automobiles today, are under scrutiny. The DOE hopes to devise an alternative engine that can run on a variety of synthetic fuels. Its research labs are working in the field of ceramics, developing a porcelain that will be capable of withstanding the extremely high heat generated by some of the alternative engine designs. The DOE is also experimenting with electric vehicles. In 1985, Ford Motor Company built the ETX-1, an experimental electric car, to supplement the DOE's research in efficient battery-powered propulsion systems.

Public Resistance to Energy Conservation

Statistics seem to suggest that the DOE's attempts at convincing the public of the importance of conservation are paying off. The rate of energy consumption has indeed dropped since 1977. It is not clear, however, whether the DOE can take all the credit. For one thing, the country's economy is growing at a much slower pace, which may account for industrial cutbacks in energy use. Also, there has been a perceptible shift from heavy industry, with its steady drain on energy supplies, toward light manufacturing and industries that offer some type of service to consumers, such as airlines and restaurants.

Perhaps more disheartening is the feeling of some critics that America's addiction to fossil fuels has not diminished since 1977. Studies have shown that people who made the most energy improvements in their homes also added new energy-consuming items that used the energy they had conserved. For example, half of the energy consumed by the average household today is used to run an automobile. Because many households now have two or more cars—the majority of which are driven each day—the added energy consumption caused by an extra automobile greatly outweighs many of the energy-saving measures that have been taken within the home—such as the installation of insulation. Since 1986, energy efficiency (a comparison of energy used with the amount of goods and services produced) has not increased, and in 1988 it actually decreased.

It appears that Americans do not want to lower their speed on the highways (40 states have passed laws increasing the speed limit on some expressways to 65 MPH), decrease the temperature in their homes during the winter, or suffer through hot summers without air conditioning. They do not want to deny themselves processed foods or stop fertilizing their lawns with synthetic chemicals, items that require huge amounts of energy to produce. Most people would rather pay more for their energy than try to conserve or cut back their consumption of it. Changing these attitudes is beyond the scope of the DOE, yet these issues must be addressed before any lasting solution to the energy problem can be found.

The Government's Fuel Reserves

The oil crises of the 1970s posed real threats to the economy and national security of the United States. The country was suddenly faced with the frightening fact that without fuel, the nation would not only shut down but would also have no means of defending itself against enemy attack. In 1975, Congress established the Strategic Petroleum Reserve (SPR) to create a basic reserve of oil so that the United States would never be as dependent on foreign supplies as it had been at the time of the Arab embargo.

The SPR has a goal of accumulating a reserve of 750 million barrels by the mid-1990s, although this figure could change based on political conditions in the Persian Gulf. When the SPR is completely filled, there will be enough oil to supply the country with 3 million barrels a day for 90 days.

By 1988, the SPR had a reserve of 550 million barrels of oil. The federal government purchased these reserves from domestic producers as well as from international dealers, such as Petróleos Mexicanos, Mexico's state-owned oil company. The SPR's inventory is held in six underground storage areas along the Texas and Louisiana coasts. The largest of these storage facilities, Bryan Mound, in Brazoria County, Texas, can hold 226 million barrels of oil.

In addition to the SPR, the government maintains the Naval Petroleum Reserves (NPR) to provide emergency oil and natural gas supplies for the national defense. Established between 1912 and 1924 through a series of executive orders, the NPR derives its resources from three federally owned oil fields: Elk Hills near Bakersfield, California; Buena Vista Hills outside Los Angeles, California; and Teapot Dome near Casper, Wyoming. In 1986, the NPR produced 43,400,105 barrels of crude oil and 130,745,641 cubic feet of natural gas.

The Phillips Petroleum terminal at Bryan Mound, Texas, where one of six underground facilities that stockpile oil for the Strategic Petroleum Reserve (SPR) is located. Congress created the SPR in 1976 to provide emergency reserves of petroleum in the event of supply disruptions in foreign oil.

International Cooperation

Because the United States cannot resolve its energy problems without the consideration and consultation of its neighbors and allies, it has taken an active role in formulating and implementing internationally agreed-upon energy policies. The DOE helps the nation's leaders develop international energy policy, and it often serves as the country's representative in international forums.

The United States maintains the closest ties with its NATO allies, which include Canada, Great Britain, France, and West Germany. The members of NATO have devised a plan to maintain an uninterrupted flow of energy supplies during major international disruptions, such as war. The allies have not only determined how much fuel would be required in such an emergency but have also drawn up the ways and means of distributing resources among themselves.

61

The DOE and the Department of State represent the United States in the International Energy Agency (IEA), an organization of 21 nations founded in 1974 to address international energy supply problems. The IEA provides a forum for countries to discuss and solve the problems of managing the world's energy supply and of developing new technologies. The ultimate goal of the IEA is to create enough energy reserves to provide for a smooth, efficient, and constant supply of fuel among its members. Methods for an early release of oil from the IEA's reserves have been achieved, and should another oil disruption occur, the IEA is confident it can avert the severe economic dislocations of the past.

IEA nations have begun to practice oil sharing by opening their markets in oil and natural gas imports to other members. The agency is studying clean-coal issues and nuclear fusion, as well as renewable energy sources. The DOE's participation in the IEA is a significant indication of the U.S. commitment to ensuring global energy security.

Acid Rain and the Greenhouse Effect

The extensive use of fossil fuels has created certain environmental problems that the DOE cannot ignore. These problems are not confined to the United States; they are international in scope.

Pollutants emitted from automobiles and from factories that burn oil and coal can cause acid rain. The DOE is conducting various studies on the effects of acid rain and, more important, on the greenhouse effect. The burning of fossil fuels and use of certain combinations of the chemicals fluorine and carbon (known as fluorocarbons), coupled with the cutting down of trees (which replenish the oxygen level) can lead to the buildup of carbon dioxide in the earth's atmosphere. The carbon dioxide acts as an umbrella, or greenhouse roof, trapping heat instead of allowing it to escape into space. An increase of carbon dioxide in the atmosphere could cause the climate to become warmer, an event that could drastically alter the earth's terrain. Between 1980 and 1986, the nation spent $150 million on studies concerning the greenhouse effect. The DOE was responsible for coordinating these studies.

In 1985, the DOE issued a report on the greenhouse effect compiled by 70 internationally respected scientists. The scientists studied regions of the earth's surface and monitored changes in climate. Their report included information on all aspects of the environment, including plants, animals, and

An ecologist at the Argonne National Laboratory in Argonne, Illinois, monitors the effects of acid rain on plant life. Pollutants contained in automobile exhaust and factory smoke are believed to be the cause of acid rain.

man. Although their study provided important information, the scientists themselves could not agree on the climatic and biological repercussions of the greenhouse effect.

The Crisis Continues

Despite the enormous tasks it faces—the dwindling fossil-fuel supply, the need for international cooperation, and the results of a century of indiscriminate pollution and misuse of the nation's energy supplies—the DOE must walk a fine line in constructing its energy policy. At once it must balance the opinions of lobbyists employed by the oil companies, of consumer activist groups (which fear higher fuel-oil prices and the weakening of laws protecting the environment), and the politics of Congress and of the president. Its success so far is a commentary on the DOE's determination and the nation's slow awakening to the crisis that, though not as acute as in the 1970s, has not gone away.

Geothermal energy such as that which pours forth from geysers is used to generate electricity. The process, however, is only economical where geothermal heat is concentrated close enough to the surface of the earth to be easily extracted.

FIVE

The Promise of Renewables

The dwindling supply and hazardous environmental effects of fossil fuels prompted the DOE to seek alternative sources of energy. It concentrated its efforts on nondepletable energy sources such as the sun, the wind, the ocean, and the earth. The fundamental characteristic of all these sources is that they can be produced indefinitely and in limitless quantity; hence they are known as renewables. In contrast to fossil fuels, renewables are clean and are as plentiful as the sun warming the nation's beaches and water bubbling up from the earth's superheated core.

The DOE and Renewable Energy

In March 1987, the DOE sent President Ronald Reagan a report entitled *Energy Security*. The report maintained that intensive research into alternative energy systems such as renewables was vital to the United States's energy security for several reasons. First, the supply of this type of fuel is limitless. Second, renewable energy sources are found throughout the United States and are not something the country would have to import. Third, they can be converted into any form of energy—electricity, heat, gas, or liquid or solid fuels—so all sectors of the nation's economy could use them. Although in 1987 the country derived only 9 percent of its energy from renewables, the report predicted that by the year 2007 this figure would increase to 12 percent.

As in all other areas of energy development, the DOE's research in renewable energy centers on high-risk or long-term technological issues that are beyond the scope of private industry. The department has limited itself to those aspects of research that are not available to the public and that are the most critical to enhancing the nation's energy security. To this end, the DOE has heavily invested in the most promising of the renewables, solar energy and geothermal energy.

Solar Energy

The DOE spends the largest share of its renewable energy budget on solar energy. In 1988, this category, which includes solar heating, solar thermal energy (a method that employs mirrors to reflect the sun's energy onto a central receiver to produce heat), photovoltaics, wind power, and ocean thermal energy, received $96.8 million.

Hundreds of mirrors in this fixed-bowl solar concentrator reflect sunlight onto the central receiver at the top of the tower. This solar thermal energy is then converted into steam, which in turn produces electricity.

Solar Heating   The sun's energy can be used to heat homes and businesses simply by utilizing the structure of the building. Thick walls, south-facing windows, concrete and foam insulation, and storage devices can trap the sun's heat during the day. The stored energy is gradually dispersed through the house at night, either by natural means or by mechanical fans or blowers.

The material of which a building is constructed can also control the amount of heat it absorbs during the summer. The DOE is developing a coating for windows that reacts to the intensity of sunlight, similar to the way some eyeglasses turn dark when the wearer goes outdoors. This film reduces the building's absorption of heat on sunny days by turning the windows opaque. On cloudy days, the windows remain clear and allow heat to penetrate the building.

Solar Thermal Energy   Electricity and heat can be produced by concentrating the sun's radiation on special, mirrored reflectors that focus sunlight onto a receiver at the top of a tower. The receiver absorbs the heat from the sun, causing water circulating through the tower to turn to steam. The steam is then used to turn a turbine, which produces electricity. This electricity is channeled to a central receiver, where it can be distributed to utility plants and, ultimately, to consumers.

Solar-power collectors have been used to heat water for local residences in California and Florida since the early 1900s. The government now plans to build collectors large enough to provide energy for whole communities. The DOE has been collaborating with universities and commercial companies to develop reflectors and concentrators (membranes applied to reflectors to trap and concentrate solar energy) to harness solar thermal energy. One of the most successful reflectors thus far is the heliostat, some models of which are as large as 450 square feet. In this design, the mirrors that reflect the sun's light are mounted along two lines, or axes. The DOE supports research in the development of chemical films that will coat the heliostat's mirrors and enhance their reflective capabilities. It has devised a thin film made of polymer or metal foil, which is lighter and cheaper than the types of coating currently in use.

Photovoltaics   Photovoltaic cells, also known as solar cells, are the most promising of all forms of solar energy. In 1988 alone, the DOE spent $35 million on photovoltaic research. These tiny solar cells, which are coated with a chemical film such as silicon, collect sunlight and then convert it directly to electricity. When light strikes the cell, electrons are released in the chemical coating and electricity is generated. Photovoltaic cells require no concentrators, storage units, or transfer equipment, and the energy they produce is immediately usable.

Although solar cells are now used to power calculators, watches, and even the Coast Guard's buoy markers at sea, at present they are still very expensive to produce and are not used extensively. Through its research the DOE is working to reduce the cost of photovoltaics. Its National Photovoltaic Program supervises the development of new materials that do not wear out after prolonged exposure to light.

Wind Power   Wind is the cheapest source of solar energy. (Wind is caused by the unequal heating of the earth's surface by the sun.) It is easily converted to electricity by means of the windmill or wind turbine. Scientists have discovered that the most effective method of producing power from wind is by using a series of small windmills with blades measuring 100 to 200 feet long. These clusters of windmills are linked together to form one plant, which is often called a wind farm. This method works far better than does a single large windmill working independently.

In 1988, the DOE allocated $17 million toward wind energy. Its Federal Wind Energy Program is studying the aerodynamics and materials of blades and the structural design of turbines that have been subjected to stress and fatigue. The DOE conducts wind energy research at three sites in the United States: the Pacific Northwest Laboratory in Richland, Washington; the Sandia National Laboratories in Albuquerque, New Mexico; and the Solar Energy Research Institute (SERI) in Golden, Colorado.

In 1986, California, the leading wind farm state, produced enough energy to equal that produced by 1 million barrels of oil. Hawaii, another developing center of wind power, is increasing its role in the industry. From 1987 to 1988 these two states combined increased their power production to 1500 megawatts, which was the same amount of energy generated by a large conventional power plant during that period.

Ocean Thermal Energy   Oceans cover 70 percent of the earth's surface. Sixty million square kilometers of water absorb enough solar energy to equal the output of 250 million barrels of oil. If the nation could convert a mere one-tenth of 1 percent of this energy to electricity, its generating capacity would increase 20 times.

The theoretical process of turning solar radiation from the world's oceans into electricity is called ocean thermal energy conversion or OTEC. This method utilizes the temperature difference between warm water from the

Scientists and engineers at the Sandia National Laboratories in Albuquerque, New Mexico, are working to develop durable, low-cost wind turbines, such as this eggbeater-shaped Darrieus wind turbine, that can be produced and marketed by the power industry. The vertical blades of the Darrieus wind turbine are shaped like the cross section of an airplane wing and can catch the wind from any direction.

ocean's surface and cold water from its depths to operate an engine that produces electricity.

The United States became interested in OTEC in the 1970s when it realized it had to develop alternative energy sources to oil. The DOE provides funding for OTEC research at the Seacoast Test Facility, located at Hawaii's National Energy Laboratory, where there is a limitless supply of warm and cold water available. The DOE hopes initially to market OTEC power to island communities, where oil is expensive and warm ocean water is plentiful. In the future, OTEC energy may be available to southern coastal cities as well. At present, however, OTEC is the most experimental of all DOE research projects.

The Chepachet, *a former U.S. naval tanker, is being converted into a test facility to evaluate the feasibility of ocean thermal energy conversion (OTEC). The OTEC process, though still theoretical, will exploit the temperature difference between warm water from the ocean's surface and cold water from its depths to generate electricity.*

Geothermal Energy

The most potentially profitable nonsolar energy source is geothermal energy—heat generated by natural processes from beneath the surface of the earth. Geothermal energy is found in steam and hot water, such as that which pours forth from geysers, and in pressurized brines containing natural gas; hot, dry rock; and magma, or molten rock. These brines erupt from the earth's fiery core where the crust is thinnest: New Zealand, New Guinea, the Philippines, Japan, western Siberia, the West Coast of the United States, South America, Mexico, and Central America. These are the volcanic lands of the so-called ring of fire or Pacific ring.

Geothermal energy has been used to heat and cool buildings, process food and other manufactured goods, and generate electricity. At one northern California power plant known as The Geysers, geothermal heat is producing enough electricity to meet the needs of about 1 million people.

In 1988, the DOE budgeted $20.9 million for geothermal energy research. At the Fenton Hill test site in New Mexico the DOE is attempting to extract heat from hot, dry rock. The most experimental of the department's geothermal programs is being conducted in a shallow lava lake in Hawaii, where DOE scientists are studying the future possibilities of magma-generated heat. The DOE is conducting a geological survey of the area to get an accurate picture of the physical characteristics and nature of the molten rock. Once the survey is completed, the department will then be able to determine whether it is financially feasible to extract heat from the lava.

The ultimate drawback to geothermal energy is that the industries drawing energy from these sources are tied to specific locations, as producers have no way of transporting the earth's energy. The geothermal industry in the United States is located mainly in California, Hawaii, Nevada, and Utah, where most geysers, hot springs, and volcanoes are found. Nevertheless, the DOE has enough confidence in the potential of geothermal energy that it has given this program more funds than any other renewable energy program except photovoltaics.

The Geysers power plant in northern California generates electricity from steam trapped beneath the earth's surface. The facility, which produces enough power to meet the needs of about 1 million people, is the only commercial geothermal power plant in the United States.

Other Renewable Energy Sources

Two other types of renewable energy come from biofuels and municipal waste and garbage. Biofuels are the end product of biomass, substances such as wood, agricultural crops, animal manure, and aquatic plants that have been treated with heat or biochemicals (living organisms such as bacteria and yeasts or their products, such as enzymes). When heat is applied to the biomass, a gas is formed; when biochemicals are applied, the biomass ferments or is digested by the biochemicals and a liquid or gas is produced.

The most common biofuels derived from biomass are alcohol and methane, a principal component in natural gas. Ethanol (ethyl alcohol), a fuel resulting from the fermentation of grains, potatoes, or other starchy plants, is frequently

A DOE researcher measures plant seedlings as part of a study of biomass fuel. The DOE is involved in many areas of biofuel research and hopes eventually to encourage the private sector to manufacture enough energy from biofuels to equal the energy produced by natural gas.

mixed with gasoline to produce the alternative automobile fuel known as gasohol.

The DOE is involved in many areas of biofuel research. Eventually it hopes to encourage the private sector to manufacture enough energy from biofuels to equal the energy produced by natural gas. The department has made significant advances toward this goal: Whereas in the 1970s energy from biofuels matched only 10 percent of the energy derived from natural gas, by the late 1980s, this figure had grown to 50 percent.

The most widely used form of biomass is wood, which can be burned directly to produce heat or processed to produce methanol, also known as wood alcohol. The DOE's Genetic Research Program is determining which hardwoods serve best as biomass. The agency has developed crops of trees that can grow from previously cut stumps and thereby decrease the time it takes to raise a forest. Five model species—black locust, poplar, silver maple, sweet gum, and cottonwood—are being grown in experimental forests. In addition to possessing the ability to grow quickly, these species have the chemical and physical characteristics to facilitate their conversion to fuels.

The DOE has extended its research in biofuels to plants and aquatic crops. In 1982, scientists discovered that microscopic algae manufacture oils that can be used in transportation fuels. Out of an initial 3,000 strains, the DOE has narrowed its field of genetic study to the 25 best strains. The price of a gallon of plant or microalgal transportation fuel has dropped from $18 in the early 1980s to $7 in 1986, and the DOE believes it can further lower the price to $1.60 a gallon.

Energy can also be obtained from garbage. First, all metal and glass must be removed from the refuse. The garbage is then burned, and the heat given off is converted to steam or electricity. A facility in Hempstead, New York, for instance, extracts 20 percent of the community's electricity from its garbage.

The Pros and Cons of Renewables

There are some drawbacks to producing energy from renewables. Foremost among them is that renewable energy is dependent on the local environment. Solar thermal energy, for example, can be obtained only on a sunny day; wind power needs a constant, reliable source of wind; and geothermal energy is applicable in only a few areas where the earth's inner heat comes quite close to the surface. The problem of storing this energy is another drawback, as is the absence of ready means necessary for combining renewable energy with

A waste-processing plant on the grounds of the Hooker Chemical Company in Niagara Falls, New York. The $74 million plant converts thousands of tons of garbage each day into fuel for electricity.

traditional sources already in use in the private and public sectors. The DOE has formed the Energy Storage Program to address these problems. It is focusing its efforts on developing storage vessels, such as batteries and electrochemicals (substances or solutions, such as zinc bromine, that conduct electric current), so that renewable energy can be retained and dispensed as needed.

The positive aspects of renewable energy, however, far outweigh the negative. In most cases, the principal cost for renewables is incurred in the construction of the power plant. The fuel itself costs nothing and takes nothing from the environment.

International Efforts in Renewable Energy

As with fossil fuels and nuclear energy, the United States and other nations share information and set policies on renewable energy. The secretary of energy chairs the Committee on Renewable Energy Commerce and Trade (CORECT), which is made up of senior officials from 12 federal agencies, among them the Department of Commerce and the Agency for International Development. Founded in 1984, CORECT is working to expand the export of renewable energy technology. In 1983, the United States exported less than $100 million worth of renewable energy technology. CORECT pinpointed the overseas markets for sale of U.S. products: biomass to the Caribbean nations and Asia; wind energy to India and China; and geothermal energy to Latin America. It publicized the government's export services and expertise that were available to commercial interests. The success of CORECT's ventures was marked: By 1987, the export of services related to renewable energy had grown to $250 million.

The DOE's involvement in the research, development, and marketing of renewable energy, although tentative in the past, has become more aggressive. The amount of money the DOE is investing in these resources strongly indicates the department's positive commitment to finding alternatives to fossil fuels and nuclear power.

A DOE employee tests the Susquehanna River for contamination shortly after the Three Mile Island nuclear power plant (in background) leaked radioactive gas into the atmosphere. The March 28, 1979, accident at the Pennsylvania facility was the worst nuclear reactor disaster in U.S. history.

SIX

Disillusionment with Nuclear Energy

Nuclear fission, or the splitting of the atom to release the energy stored within, seemed a promising energy source for post–World War II America. The supply was almost infinite and the power cheap to produce. In reality, however, nuclear power plants were so inefficient that the uranium fuel supply was in danger of being depleted as quickly as the fossil-fuel supply. Moreover, the American public could not overcome a deep mistrust of nuclear energy, a nagging fear that surfaced after the disasters at the Three Mile Island and Chernobyl nuclear power plants.

Three Mile Island and Chernobyl

On March 28, 1979, a failure in the cooling system of the Unit 2 reactor at the Three Mile Island (TMI) nuclear power plant in Pennsylvania caused the uranium-filled core of the reactor to overheat and begin to melt. A small amount of radioactive gas was released into the atmosphere, forcing many people to evacuate the area temporarily. The Nuclear Regulatory Commission's study of the accident concluded that TMI "was designed without a central concept of man-machine integration." In other words, people could not operate TMI safely or efficiently. TMI workers were responsible for 2,000 controls and 1,500 warning alarms, many of which were hard or impossible to see and read. For example, the indicator light that warned that a valve on Unit 2's pressurized containment vessel was open and that cooling water was boiling away was located on the back of the control panel where the operator could not see it.

Seven years later and halfway around the world, another nuclear accident occurred at the Chernobyl nuclear power plant in the Soviet Union. On April 26, 1986, Soviet operators experimented with a turbo-generator in the fourth reactor unit without taking adequate safety measures. Two explosions, only seconds apart, damaged the reactor containment building, spewed radioactive fragments into the air, and pelted the plant with graphite from the reactor's core that was hot enough to set fires. The plant's entire safety control system was destroyed immediately.

The Soviets fought the fire and delayed evacuating the 1,000 workers and 135,000 people living within approximately 19 miles of the plant. Thirty-one people died as a result of the accident, and the long-term effects of radiation exposure on the local population and neighboring European countries will only be known in years to come.

The accidents at both TMI and Chernobyl were the result of human error and inexperience. The Soviet Union, which had invested more heavily in nuclear power than had the United States, had built plants faster than it could train the personnel to run them. And Soviet engineers, like their American counterparts, had not taken into account the needs of the people operating the plants. Mechanical and design flaws at the Chernobyl plant clearly revealed an engineering failure to perceive the importance of the "human factor" in preventing tragic nuclear accidents.

The DOE gained useful information from the TMI and Chernobyl tragedies. Although the cleanup of the reactor at TMI was left to the owner, the General Public Utilities Nuclear Corporation (and cost an estimated $900 million), DOE personnel recovered data from the plant on safety problems, the defueling (removal of used atomic fuel) of nuclear reactors, the progression of damage through a reactor core, and the manufacture of containers for shipping radioactive waste to storage dumps. The gravity and magnitude of the Chernobyl disaster led the DOE to reassess its nuclear reactor safety guidelines and tighten its safety standards. The conclusions reached by the DOE as a result of these two incidents prompted the federal government to revise its rules governing commercial nuclear power plants. The Nuclear Regulatory Commission strengthened its regulation of nuclear power plants, and construction permits for new plants became more difficult to obtain.

The DOE's research also brought the flaws in both U.S. and foreign reactors to the country's attention. In 1985, the department launched an effort to

Soviet health specialists in Kiev check produce for radiation contamination in the aftermath of the April 1986 accident at the Chernobyl nuclear power plant. Countries throughout Europe were exposed to radiation released from the damaged plant, which is located about 80 miles north of Kiev.

revitalize the nation's nuclear power industry, which was floundering under the weight of safety legislation, public mistrust, and a lack of cost-effectiveness. It chose six contractors, including General Electric and Westinghouse, to design and test light-water reactors to meet standardized requirements. These companies are working to develop one uniform reactor design that meets all of the government's safety requirements. This standardized design would eventually replace a multiplicity of reactor designs now in use. The DOE hopes that its advances in this area will help allay the country's fears about nuclear power and will bring about the removal of legislative limitations on the design and environmental restrictions of nuclear power plants.

To minimize human error in nuclear accidents, the DOE has investigated fault-tolerant computers that can run highly automated plant systems and override incorrect information responsible for reactor shutdowns. "Smart-sensors," which will not send faulty signals and thus avert reactor outages, can also help diagnose problems in the operational system. Finally, the DOE is promoting the use of robots for jobs that have a high risk of radiation contamination.

The DOE has formulated a plan for civilian evacuation of communities in the vicinity of nuclear power plants and is working on strategies to warn and remove endangered populations in more distant locales. It is also devoting a significant amount of resources to the development of specially designed fire-fighting equipment for use in battling a nuclear blaze.

The International Atomic Energy Agency

The United States is an active member of the International Atomic Energy Agency (IAEA), an organization of 113 nations founded in 1957 to promote the peaceful use of nuclear energy and prevent the spread of nuclear explosive devices. The secretary of energy heads the U.S. delegation to the IAEA, which meets annually in Vienna, Austria. In 1986 and again in 1987, the main focus of the IAEA's general conference was the Chernobyl accident. During the 1986 conference Soviet experts submitted a detailed account of the accident and its effects in the Soviet Union. They continued to blame human

Members of the International Atomic Energy Agency (IAEA) attend a special meeting held in Vienna, Austria, in May 1986 to discuss proposals for improving nuclear safety and cooperation, the importance of which was highlighted by the Chernobyl disaster one month earlier. Founded in 1957, the IAEA works to promote the peaceful use of nuclear energy and to prevent the spread of nuclear explosive devices.

At the DOE's Oak Ridge National Laboratory in Oak Ridge, Tennessee, researchers are studying the biological effects of radiation on mice. Experiments involving hundreds of thousands of mice over the course of 30 years have provided the U.S. government with valuable information on the cell damage that radiation causes in mammals.

error for the disaster, but they also admitted that their reactor design was flawed and lacked safeguards against such operator mistakes as the one that had caused the accident. At the conference the IAEA agreed to establish centers in Atlanta, Moscow, Paris, and Tokyo to gather information and coordinate emergency assistance in the event of a nuclear accident.

Much of the discussion at the 1987 IAEA conference focused on the effects of radiation contamination on human beings and the environment. The incidents at both TMI and Chernobyl have revealed how vulnerable all nations are to nuclear accidents. The effects of radiation are both immediate and long term. Exposure to high levels of radiation can cause burns, disfigurement, and even death. Radiation can alter or mutate human genes, resulting in cancer, disease, and birth defects. Often genetic damage and undetected illnesses caused by radiation contamination are not immediately apparent and are only revealed in future generations.

In 1986, after the Chernobyl disaster, the IAEA initiated special studies on the long-term health effects of radiation. DOE researchers are often called on to contribute to these studies. Their work in developing tests for early detection of radiation-related diseases—as well as in ways of correcting cell damage after it has occurred—has provided the IAEA with valuable information.

Although the IAEA supports the free exchange of nuclear technology for peaceful purposes, it believes that trade in this technology must be strictly monitored and regulated so that the destructive nature of nuclear energy is not misused. Because nuclear technology can be used to proliferate, or produce more, nuclear weapons, member nations must sign the Treaty on the Nonproliferation of Nuclear Weapons, in which they agree not to sell commercial nuclear technology to nations that have not signed the treaty. The treaty also sets guidelines for nonproliferation. First, IAEA members use only low-enriched fuels in their reactors—that is, fuels with 20 percent or less uranium. Although this regulation has forced some members to redesign their reactors, it has strengthened the security of nuclear energy: Smaller quantities of uranium are easier to protect and monitor. Second, member nations have agreed to exchange technical information and share expertise to help avoid future nuclear mishaps.

In carrying out its role as the government's agent in regulating nuclear technology exports and negotiating treaties concerning the peaceful use of nuclear energy, the DOE maintains close contact with the IAEA. DOE personnel frequently participate in IAEA-sponsored symposia and international research groups. Together both agencies strive to give to the world all the benefits of nuclear energy without subjecting it to all the dangers.

Nuclear Waste Disposal

The uncontrolled release of radioactive material into the surrounding environment could pose a major source of pollution and contamination of the land, water, and air. The DOE decontaminates areas polluted by its own facilities. Sometimes, when it is not clear who is responsible for the cleanup of a decontaminated area or when a state does not have a designated disposal site, the DOE is called in to decontaminate privately owned facilities.

Another potential source of nuclear contamination is the improper disposal of nuclear waste. Most nuclear waste produced by power plants, research institutions, and hospitals (radioactive materials are used to treat various diseases, such as some forms of cancer) are classified as low level—that is, they emit only a small amount of radiation and generally are not dangerous to

Low-level nuclear waste from various DOE defense projects is packed in crates and buried in trenches at the Nevada Test Site near Las Vegas. Nuclear material that is classified as low level emits only a small amount of radiation and generally is not dangerous to handlers.

handlers. The DOE advises state and local governments on methods of disposing of this type of waste and occasionally rebates a portion of the disposal fee when the organizations reach a certain point in the cleanup process.

The disposal of high-level nuclear waste, such as spent, or used, nuclear fuel, is the exclusive domain of the DOE. The department's Office of Civilian Radioactive Waste Management, which was established under the Nuclear Waste Policy Act of 1982, oversees the construction of underground storage depositories. By 1998, the DOE hopes to have in place a system of monitored retrievable storage facilities where nuclear waste can be treated and processed before being transported to a permanent site. The proposed sites for these intermediate storage dumps are in Tennessee. However, the state of Tennessee has filed a suit against the DOE to stop the proposal, and construction has been delayed until the Supreme Court can hear the case.

Similar problems arose in 1986 when President Reagan designated a number of sites for permanent storage of nuclear waste. After preliminary environmental assessments, seismic surveys, and exploratory drilling, Hanford, Washington; Deaf County in Texas; and the Yucca mountain region of Nevada were selected. Native Americans living on the land, including the Nez Perce, the Yakima Indian Nation, and the Confederated Tribes of the Umatilla Indian Reservation, refused to accept the designation. They have united with the states involved to block further DOE action through litigation, and the problem of what to do with the nuclear waste generated in the country each day has yet to be solved.

Theoretical Research

The DOE recognizes the need for purely theoretical research to serve as a foundation for the expansion and improvement of its nuclear energy program. In the United States, 90 percent of all high-energy physics and 80 percent of all nuclear physics (the study of nuclear structure) are funded by the DOE. The theoretical sciences of high-energy and nuclear physics probe energy at the level of subatomic particles and forces, which are the building blocks of the

The main accelerator tunnel at the Fermi National Accelerator Laboratory in Batavia, Illinois, where physicists are working to construct the super grand unifying theory. The aim of the theory is to describe the interaction of all matter and energy in the universe.

universe. All modern science and technology derive from an understanding of the fundamental components of matter and energy forms and from the natural laws that govern their relationships.

High-Energy Physics

The DOE defines high-energy physics as the identification of the "basic building blocks of matter and the fundamental nature of the forces that act between them." Physicists hope to devise a theoretical framework that unites the four elemental forces of nature: the strong force, which holds particles in the nucleus together; the weak force, which causes nuclear decay; the electromagnetic force, which binds molecules and atoms together; and the gravitational force, which pulls all matter toward other matter. This theory, known as the super grand unifying theory, will describe the interaction of all matter and energy in the universe. It will re-create the moment before the universe was formed, when all the forces were united.

Scientists at three national facilities funded by the DOE—the Fermi National Accelerator Laboratory in Batavia, Illinois; the Stanford Linear Accelerator Center at Stanford University in California; and the Brookhaven National Laboratory in Upton, New York—are working to reproduce this moment. High-energy particle accelerators at each facility can produce the collision speed necessary for the combining of subatomic particles, and thus simulate conditions that existed close to the beginning of time.

Nuclear Physics

Nuclear physics concerns the structure and behavior of the nuclei of atoms, the basic elements of all matter. The DOE's Nuclear Physics Program constructs and tests scientific models of the nucleus and the way it acts. Seven DOE test facilities throughout the United States are equipped with accelerators that thrust beams of protons (positively charged subatomic particles), electrons (negatively charged subatomic particles), or other particles on targets of stable nuclei. When the beam strikes the nuclei it produces a nuclear reaction. These reactions are studied and provide valuable information on the interaction of nuclear particles.

In 1987, the DOE began construction of the Continuous Electron Beam Accelerator Facility in Newport News, Virginia. The facility, which is scheduled to open in 1993, will provide precise beams of electrons that will open up the structure of protons and neutrons (uncharged subatomic particles) in the nucleus so that scientists can investigate the underlying structures of these particles. The new knowledge gained from this facility, which is the first of its type in the world, should lead to an even more sophisticated understanding of the construction and behavior of matter.

Fusion

Magnetic fusion, or the uniting of two or more nuclei, though still theoretical, may be a practical energy source in the near future. Fusion occurs naturally in the sun and other stars and is the basic producer of energy in the universe. The fusion reaction, first described by Albert Einstein in 1907 as $E = mc^2$, (in which E = energy, m = mass, and c = the velocity of light) is the result of the union of the nuclei of light elements to form the nucleus of a heavier element. In the process, some of the mass of the nuclei is changed into energy.

The fusion reaction requires intense heat and pressure to unite the nuclei, which are positively charged and naturally repel each other. Today, scientists can produce this reaction only in the hydrogen bomb. The splitting, or fission, of uranium atoms creates an explosion and temporarily raises the temperature high enough to fuse the hydrogen nuclei. This is uncontrolled and destructive fusion, not usable in a power plant. The dream is to harness this energy safely.

In order for fusion to occur, a collision speed close to the speed of light and a temperature of 100 million degrees centigrade (1,800,032 degrees Fahrenheit) must be achieved. At the DOE-supported Princeton Plasma Physics Laboratory in Princeton, New Jersey, scientists are attempting to induce the fusion reaction in a special accelerator, the Tokamak Fusion Test Reactor. Although they have achieved the necessary speed and temperature for fusion, these conditions have not occurred together, which is essential for the reaction to take place.

The DOE is particularly interested in fusion because it could supply a limitless amount of energy that is environmentally safe. Unlike nuclear fission, which requires rare metals such as uranium and plutonium for fuel, fusion uses hydrogen, which is plentiful. Fission burns large quantities of fuel, and uncontrolled reactions are possible. Fusion uses small amounts of hydrogen, and no dangerous reactions can occur. Fusion manufactures no radioactive dust, only helium, and yields 10 times as much energy as fission.

Defense-Related Activities in Nuclear Energy

The research and development of nuclear weaponry is vital to the security of the country. The DOE contributes to the nation's defense by performing

The Tokamak Fusion Test Reactor at the Princeton Plasma Physics Laboratory at Princeton University, where research on fusion is being carried out. The DOE is particularly interested in fusion because the energy it produces is limitless and environmentally safe.

weapons research at the Lawrence Livermore National Laboratory in Livermore, California; the Los Alamos National Laboratory in Los Alamos, New Mexico; and the Sandia National Laboratories in Albuquerque, New Mexico and Livermore, California. It also carries out the testing of these weapons at the Nevada Test Site near Las Vegas and is responsible for any damage done during the testing process.

Since 1977, the DOE has managed the government's medical, radiological, and environmental programs in the Marshall Islands in the central Pacific. Between 1946 and 1958, the United States conducted extensive nuclear weapons tests in this area. The tests, which forced more than 300 inhabitants to leave their native lands, devastated portions of the Eniwetok and Bikini atolls (ring-shaped coral reefs that appear above the surface of water). One explosion on March 1, 1954, exposed 82 Marshallese to high levels of radioactive fallout. As a result of this incident the Atomic Energy Commission began providing medical aid to the islanders in 1955. The DOE took over this responsibility when it absorbed the Energy Research and Development Administration

Inhabitants of Bikini Atoll load their belongings onto a U.S. Navy ship as they prepare to evacuate their native land in March 1946. Between 1946 and 1958, the United States conducted extensive nuclear weapons tests on both Bikini and Eniwetok atolls in the central Pacific.

(which had replaced the Atomic Energy Commission in 1974). The DOE also monitors the environment of the islands, evaluating the soil and plant life for contamination, so that eventually the islanders can be resettled to their ancestral lands.

In addition to the research, development, and testing of nuclear weapons, the DOE is involved in the manufacture of these armaments. The department employs outside contractors to operate seven government-owned nuclear weapons plants. These plants produce nuclear warheads and bombs for the army, navy, and air force, including warheads for the navy's Trident missile system and the army's Pershing missile system.

Various weapons plants under the supervision of the DOE manufacture materials used in the production of nuclear warheads. Soon after the Chernobyl accident in 1986, the department began an investigation of the Hanford nuclear weapons plant in Washington State, which produced plutonium and tritium and was similar in design to the Soviet reactor that had exploded. As a result, the DOE closed the Hanford reactor for extensive safety modifications.

In the fall of 1988, reports of dangerous practices and near disasters at two other weapons plants surfaced publicly. In early October, the E.I. du Pont de Nemours and Company, which built and operates the government-owned Savannah River nuclear weapons plant near Aiken, South Carolina, admitted that approximately 30 "significant" reactor incidents had occurred over the 28-year history of the plant. Although no disaster of the magnitude of Chernobyl or TMI had occurred at the Savannah River Plant (SRP), the mishaps there included leaks in the reactor core's cooling system, the melting of nuclear fuel, and radioactive contamination.

The Savannah River Plant was built in 1952 in the middle of the cold war, when tensions between the United States and the Soviet Union escalated to a position just short of war. At that time, the United States was confronting what it perceived as a constant military threat from the Soviet Union. As a result,

(continued on page 93)

The DOE's Savannah River Plant near Aiken, South Carolina, produces the nuclear fuel tritium for the military's nuclear warheads. The plant was the focus of congressional hearings held in October 1988, at which time it was publicly disclosed that numerous nuclear accidents had occurred at the facility over its 28-year history.

America's Nuclear Submarines

Through its Naval Reactors Development Program, the DOE helps design, develop, test, and evaluate nuclear reactors for the U.S. Navy's nuclear submarine force. When the atomic submarine was first proposed in the 1940s, however, the Atomic Energy Commission (AEC), one of the DOE's forebears, did not initially agree with the navy on the need for applying nuclear power to naval propulsion. It was only through the persistent efforts of Vice Admiral Earle Mills, chief of the Bureau of Ships, and Captain Hyman G. Rickover, chief of the navy's Nuclear Power Branch, that the proposed nuclear submarine program gained the backing of Congress. In 1949, Rickover was chosen to head the AEC's Naval Reactor Branch in addition to his position with the navy.

His job: to direct the development and construction of the world's first atomic submarine. (Rickover headed the Naval Reactor Branch, which was transferred to the DOE in 1977, until he retired from the navy in 1982.)

In 1954, the USS *Nautilus* (SSN-571), the first nuclear-powered submarine, was launched. Its appearance ushered in a new era in submarine technology: Now a vessel could remain submerged indefinitely, limited only by the endurance of its crew. This was the type of ship navies the world over had sought ever since the Germans had first used submarines in World War I (1914–18).

Before the advent of nuclear power, submarines had relied on oil-powered diesel engines and elec-

The nuclear submarine USS Michigan *under construction at Groton, Connecticut.*

tric motors to propel them through the water. Diesel engines were used to drive the vessel when it was not submerged. Electric motors, which drew their power from a large complement of storage batteries located deep within various portions of the ship's hull, took over when the boat plunged beneath the waves. (After 1941, diesel engines were used as generator engines—rather than actual propulsion systems—to provide power to electric motors, which then propelled the vessel through the water.)

Until the early 1950s, the vessels in the navy's submarine force could barely make 10 knots while submerged and only 20 knots on the surface. (A knot is equal to 1.15 MPH.) These boats were actually "submersibles," rather than submarines, because they depended heavily on contact with the surface. The electric batteries required for submerged operation lost their power quickly, and the vessel's diesel engines were used to recharge them. But because diesels needed air to operate and produced exhaust gases, recharging took place on the surface. Thus, before nuclear power was developed, submersibles had to surface frequently.

The only exception to this rule came when the Germans created the schnorkel during World War II (1939–45). This tubular device allowed the submarine to cruise just below the surface while both drawing air from the atmosphere and expelling exhaust.

After the successful harnessing of fission energy in the 1940s, nuclear power provided the first opportunity to build a submarine that could remain submerged for an unlimited period of time. Unlike the earlier submersibles, the nuclear propulsion system created for the *Nautilus* neither required air from the surface nor produced any exhaust.

In a submarine nuclear propulsion system, the reactor core, containing enriched uranium in a pressure vessel, gives off energy in the form of heat. The primary cooling system, employing fast-flowing water under pressure, absorbs the heat generated by fission in the reactor core. The heat is then converted into steam, which turns a turbine, propelling the vessel and providing auxiliary power generation.

The casing for the nuclear fuel is constructed of a protective metal such as zirconium, which becomes the medium for passing heat to the water coolant as the coolant makes one or more loops through the core. The water coolant also acts as a moderator to slow the fission process to a level at which the amount of heat generated can be efficiently converted into steam to drive the vessel's turbine engines. Control rods made of a neutron-absorbing metal, such as hafnium, can also be mechanically extended into the reactor core as an additional way of controlling the nuclear reaction. These control rods also allow the submarine's engineering officer to stop the reaction entirely, if necessary.

With the *Nautilus* and the succeeding three boats of the USS *Skate* class, which incorporated slight

The mammoth USS Ohio *is almost as long as two football fields.*

changes in hull and reactor designs, the navy perfected the installation and operation of submarine nuclear propulsion systems. Soon after this was achieved, the operational capability of the American nuclear submarine took a giant leap forward when nuclear power was combined with a special hull design. In 1954, the Portsmouth Navy Shipyard in Portsmouth, New Hampshire, built the conventional, nonnuclear submarine USS *Albacore* (AGSS-569). This vessel's hull was shaped like a very slender teardrop. The flat deck of previous hull designs had been replaced by an entirely concave surface that was completely smooth. The *Albacore* proved so fast and maneuverable while submerged that the navy quickly moved to combine this hull design with an improved version of the *Nautilus*'s nuclear propulsion system.

The navy successfully combined these two features in the USS *Skipjack* (SSN-585), the prototype of all modern American submarines, and its five sister ships, launched between 1958 and 1960. These vessels could reach speeds in excess of 30 knots submerged. The navy now had submarines that could, while submerged, outrun and outmaneuver any surface vessel that might attack them.

Since the creation of the USS *Skipjack*, all American submarines have been built with a nuclear propulsion system and a teardrop hull design. This combination proved so successful that the first American ballistic missile submarine, the USS *George Washington* (SSBN-598), was built in 1959–60 by actually cutting a *Skipjack*-class vessel in half and installing a special section with tubular containers for 16 Polaris missiles. On July 20, 1960, the Polaris model A-1 became the first missile ever launched from a submerged submarine.

The latest additions to the American nuclear fleet of the 1980s are the *Los Angeles*–class attack submarines and the mammoth 19,000-ton *Ohio*-class ballistic missile submarines. These submarines can attain speeds of approximately 30 knots submerged and sustain these speeds almost indefinitely.

Now the DOE is working with the U.S. Navy to develop the Advanced Fleet Reactor that will provide a nuclear propulsion system that is quieter and more powerful than current nuclear submarine reactors. This new reactor will be the energy source behind the next generation of nuclear-powered attack submarines.

(continued from page 89)

the SRP was shrouded in secrecy and encased in security measures to protect the radioactive elements it manufactured from theft.

Over the years, the SRP remained free from outside supervision: It was answerable to no other agency except the DOE and Du Pont. It was not required to follow the rules for nuclear safety that were laid down by the NRC or institute the changes made by the rest of the industry after the TMI and Chernobyl disasters.

At congressional hearings held in October 1988 to investigate allegations of unsafe practices at the facility, a picture of an old, outmoded nuclear weapons plant that had not kept pace with industry changes emerged. Many members of Congress believed that the SRP was too dangerous to run. Among the violations disclosed at the hearings were that the plant's fire-fighting equipment consisted of garden hoses, that coolant pipes were corroding, and that gaskets in the diesel pumps leaked.

The abuses noted at the SRP seemed minor unless taken as a whole. The most serious charges were that outside inspectors were ignored when they criticized the SRP and that the DOE and Du Pont were not communicating their concerns and problems to each other. The congressional hearings forced the DOE to review the plant's operation. The DOE ordered a cutback in service until an engineering analysis could be completed, something that would not be tolerated in the commercial nuclear power industry, where no reactor may be used until the evaluation is performed.

Even more serious charges have been leveled against the DOE in regard to its management of the Feed Materials Production Center in Fernald, Ohio. The plant, located 18 miles northwest of Cincinnati, was built in 1951 under circumstances similar to the SRP.

Like all federal reactors, the Ohio plant has no containment dome to prevent the discharge of radiation into the atmosphere. On October 14, 1988, the DOE admitted that it had known since 1951 that radioactive pollution was being released into the Ohio air. Because air filters at the plant had not worked properly, at least 200,000 pounds of uranium oxide—3,000 pounds between 1980 and 1985 alone—had escaped into the atmosphere. Governor Richard F. Celeste expressed the outrage of the citizens of Ohio in a letter to President Reagan: "This admission of deceit and mismanagement confirms and emphasizes what we have known in Ohio for a long time: This facility is an environmental disaster threatening the health and safety of thousands of Ohioans."

Governor Celeste proceeded to demand that the plant be shut down. He asked the DOE to bring in outside evaluators to test employees and local residents for radiation contamination. He pointed to two storage silos that were deteriorating and in need of being cleaned up and pleaded with the DOE to treat and stabilize the radioactive thorium in the plant. Although the plant is still operating, the DOE has decided to phase out the facility and eventually close it.

The Hanford and Savannah River plants produced plutonium and tritium for America's nuclear arsenal. Although there is no pressing need for more plutonium because the number of nuclear warheads has diminished and new ones are armed with plutonium taken from the old, tritium is another matter. Tritium is the booster for the explosive power of a nuclear warhead, and it decays at a rate of about five percent a year. Twenty years without production of tritium could disarm the United States, hence the necessity of putting the nation's federal reactors back in working order.

International Efforts at Arms Control

The DOE is helping the nation verify compliance with arms control treaties, such as the Intermediate-Range Nuclear Forces (INF) Treaty signed by President Ronald Reagan and Soviet leader Mikhail Gorbachev in December 1987. The department maintains its own intelligence-gathering operation to monitor nuclear testing all over the globe. Through government-owned satellites and instruments that are commonly used to detect earthquakes and other surface disturbances, the DOE can track the movement of nuclear weapons.

Strategic Defense Initiative

President Reagan's proposed Strategic Defense Initiative (SDI) has given the DOE's nuclear program a new focus. The SDI, as formulated in 1983, requires the DOE to develop lightweight nuclear power systems for antimissile systems that have a life span of seven years of continuous use. The air force is attempting to develop a similar nonnuclear power pack under the SDI guidelines. In conjuction with the Department of Defense, the DOE is working on a nuclear power system to fuel a constellation of satellites that will determine the timing of an American response to nuclear attack.

An artist's conception of a space-based particle beam weapon attacking enemy intercontinental ballistic missiles. As part of their research supporting the Strategic Defense Initiative, or "Star Wars" program, scientists at the Los Alamos National Laboratory are working to develop a number of space-based defensive weapons.

The Future of Nuclear Energy

The promise of nuclear fission has been tarnished over the last decade by poor management and faulty design of power facilities, tragic mishaps, and lack of public support. Fusion energy appears to be a bright alternative if it can be transferred from theory into reality. Despite the obstacles to full utilization that may seem overwhelming at present, the energy inside the atom must not be overlooked in the future.

The architect of the Citicorp Center in New York City, which was constructed in 1977, at one time considered placing solar panels on the building's angled roof. The plan was rejected, however, when the project was found to be financially prohibitive.

SEVEN

The Moral Equivalent of War

In the years since its founding in 1977, the DOE has subtly changed its role in government. President Jimmy Carter realized that the way to counter threats to the nation's energy supplies was to establish a department that would foster research to increase domestic energy sources and that would coordinate a federal energy conservation program. In his April 1977 address he said, "This difficult effort will be the 'moral equivalent of war,' except that we will be uniting our efforts to build and not destroy."

President Carter perceived the DOE as a superagency capable of tackling the energy crisis and managing a headstrong industry that was abusing energy supplies and failing to adequately dispose of hazardous wastes. In the 1980s, under President Ronald Reagan, the DOE deregulated much of the energy industry, in the hope that the free market would eliminate price gouging and wasteful consumption on its own. In the 1990s, the DOE will have to seek a balance between total control of a changing energy industry and misguided permissiveness.

Perhaps the most pressing problem facing the DOE in the 1990s will be reconstructing the government-owned but privately run nuclear weapons plants. The near-disasters at the Ohio and Savannah River plants and the forced shutdown of the Hanford plant have strained the nation's defense system and have caused Americans to become deeply suspicious of the DOE's ability to safeguard the public's safety. President George Bush's secretary of energy, Admiral James D. Watkins, said in his Senate confirmation hearings in March 1989 that correcting the problems at the DOE's nuclear weapons plants would be his first priority. Under Secretary Watkins, the DOE may take a firmer stand on behalf of the nation's—and the people's—health and welfare.

The DOE has focused energy research and commercial ventures on the most productive and promising areas. It continues to support research and development in all fields relating to energy and to offer companies and individuals financial aid and technical expertise. The DOE has become a kind of north star pointing toward the most potentially rewarding energy endeavors.

The DOE is a major advocate of theoretical research in high-energy and nuclear physics. It intends to construct a superconducting supercollider in Waxahachie, Texas, and plans to have the facility completed by 1997. The supercollider, with a circumference of 53 miles, will be the largest and most expensive scientific tool ever built, costing an estimated $4.4 billion. Twenty times more powerful than any other particle accelerator, the racetrack-shaped supercollider will hurdle protons around its track at near light speed and crash them into each other. For a moment, the intensity of energy released will be equal to that created at the birth of the universe. The atoms that have been smashed will spin off particles that scientists will then be able to study.

Although exciting developments and discoveries have been made in nuclear research, the problems involving fossil fuels have not been solved. The basic question of how much fuel is left still has no answer. Most of the data available on fuel supplies come from oil and natural gas industries and are not always accurate.

The DOE has implored the American public and industries to conserve energy and has offered many ways by which to do so. For industry, conservation means changing technology and procedures to cut energy demand. For the public, conservation means avoiding gas-guzzling cars and unnecessary trips, choosing energy-efficient air conditioners, refrigerators, and other appliances, and insulating their homes. Conservation also requires switching fuels, using coal instead of oil, solar heat instead of gas, and photovoltaics instead of oil-produced electricity. Probably the most disagreeable aspect of conservation is curtailment. Lowering the thermostat, foregoing processed foods, riding a bike to work—these are measures most Americans find difficult to embrace. The DOE has studied the implications of all these measures and has kept at the public, urging it to fight energy waste.

James D. Watkins, the sixth person to hold the post of secretary of energy. At Senate confirmation hearings held in March 1989, Admiral Watkins, a former cruiser and nuclear submarine commander in the U.S. Navy, said that correcting the problems at the DOE's nuclear weapons plants would be his first priority as secretary.

At the Doublet III-D vacuum vessel in La Jolla, California, Japanese and U.S. scientists carry out joint research on fusion. The interior of the doughnut-shaped vessel is shown here.

In the 1980s, the United States joined other nations in exploring new solutions to energy problems. In 1983, the United States and the People's Republic of China signed an accord to work together on magnetic fusion and nuclear physics by sharing the expertise of their scientists. In 1987, the United States completed a 10-year program with Japan, Switzerland, and other countries to test 6 superconducting magnets at the International Fusion Superconducting Test Facility at the Oak Ridge National Laboratory in Tennessee. The DOE and the French Center for Atomic Energy signed an agreement in May 1987 to participate in joint experiments on France's advanced superconducting magnet, Tore Supra. And the United States has begun to discuss joint planning and research with the Soviet Union in the area of nuclear fusion.

The DOE is still developing its identity and a sense of what the public wants it to do. If the DOE succeeds in defining its role, then it will be able to fulfill the wish proclaimed by President Reagan on Energy Education Day 1987: "As we approach the 1990s, America must be prepared to formulate energy policy with boldness and vision." Surely, without boldness and vision in the 1990s, Americans will be doomed to relive the harsh energy realities of the 1970s.

100

Department of Energy

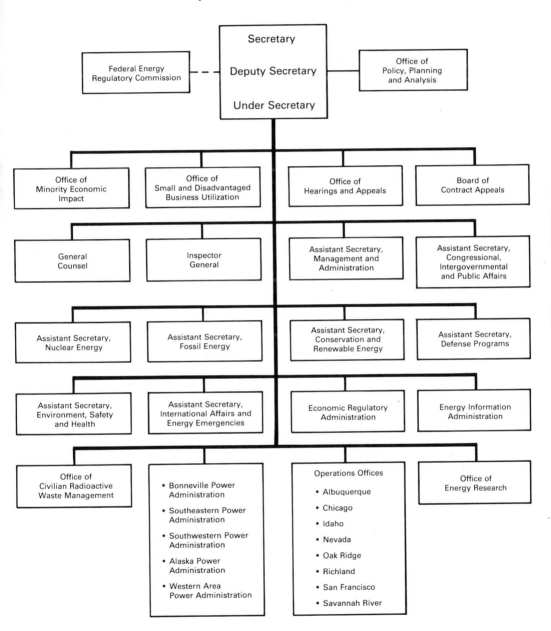

	Federal Energy Regulatory Commission	**Secretary** **Deputy Secretary** **Under Secretary**	**Office of Policy, Planning and Analysis**

Office of Minority Economic Impact	Office of Small and Disadvantaged Business Utilization	Office of Hearings and Appeals	Board of Contract Appeals
General Counsel	Inspector General	Assistant Secretary, Management and Administration	Assistant Secretary, Congressional, Intergovernmental and Public Affairs
Assistant Secretary, Nuclear Energy	Assistant Secretary, Fossil Energy	Assistant Secretary, Conservation and Renewable Energy	Assistant Secretary, Defense Programs
Assistant Secretary, Environment, Safety and Health	Assistant Secretary, International Affairs and Energy Emergencies	Economic Regulatory Administration	Energy Information Administration

Office of Civilian Radioactive Waste Management

- Bonneville Power Administration
- Southeastern Power Administration
- Southwestern Power Administration
- Alaska Power Administration
- Western Area Power Administration

Operations Offices

- Albuquerque
- Chicago
- Idaho
- Nevada
- Oak Ridge
- Richland
- San Francisco
- Savannah River

Office of Energy Research

GLOSSARY

Acid precipitation   Highly acidic rain, snow, or hail that is believed to be caused by pollutants emitted in the burning of high-sulfur coal and the operation of automobiles. Acid rain kills vegetation, poisons bodies of water, and seeps into the soil, changing its chemical balance.

Biomass   Substances such as wood, agricultural crops, and animal manure that, when treated with heat, pressure, or chemicals, produce a gaseous or liquid fuel.

Fission   The splitting of the nucleus of an atom to release energy. This type of nuclear energy is produced in commercial power plants that are regulated by the U.S. government.

Fluorocarbons   Chemical compounds made from fluorine and carbon that, when released, damage the atmosphere. These compounds are commonly used as propellants for such things as aerosol deodorants and hair sprays and are also used in industry.

Geothermal energy   Heat generated by natural processes from steam, hot water, and pressurized brines trapped beneath the earth's surface.

Greenhouse effect   The warming of the earth's atmosphere caused by the buildup of carbon dixoide, which traps heat instead of allowing it to escape into space. An increase in carbon dioxide in the atmosphere could drastically alter the earth's terrain.

Heliostat   A type of reflector used in solar energy production consisting of large mirrors mounted along two axes. These mirrors reflect the sun's rays onto a central receiver, which converts the solar energy into electricity.

High-energy physics   The identification and study of subatomic particles, the basic building blocks of matter, and the forces that act between them. The goal of high-energy-physics research is to devise a theory that will explain this interaction.

International Atomic Energy Agency (IAEA)   A 113-nation organization founded in 1957 to promote the peaceful use of nuclear energy and prevent the spread of nuclear explosive devices. The U.S. delegation to the IAEA is headed by the secretary of energy.

International Energy Agency (IEA) An organization of 21 nations, founded in 1974 to address international energy supply problems. The DOE and the Department of State represent the United States in the IEA.

Magnetic fusion The uniting of atomic nuclei at high speed and temperature, during which energy is released. At present, this process occurs only in the sun.

North Atlantic Treaty Organization (NATO) An alliance of western democracies, including the United States, Great Britain, Canada, and West Germany, that was formed after World War II to counter the growing power of the Soviet Union and its allies.

Nuclear physics The study of the structure and behavior of atomic nuclei. Fission and magnetic fusion are the main areas of this form of research.

Nuclear Regulatory Commission (NRC) A government agency independent of the DOE that oversees the operation of and sets standards for privately owned nuclear power plants.

Ocean thermal energy conversion (OTEC) A theoretical method of converting solar energy to electricity by exploiting the temperature difference between warm water from the ocean's surface and cold water from its depths.

Photovoltaics Tiny, chemically coated cells that trap sunlight and convert the solar energy directly into electricity. Photovoltaic cells are also known as solar cells.

Radon A radioactive gas formed naturally beneath the earth's surface. Radon can be harmful if it accumulates in buildings and homes, where heavy insulation sometimes prevents proper ventilation.

Strategic Defense Initiative (SDI) A theoretical weapons system that may be able to destroy an incoming nuclear missile in space. The SDI is also referred to as the Star Wars system because of its use of laser technology.

Super grand unifying theory A theory that physicists believe will explain the interaction of the basic forces in the universe. The theory will recreate the moment before the universe was formed, when all forces were united.

SELECTED REFERENCES

Barnet, Richard J. *The Lean Years: Politics in the Age of Scarcity*. New York: Simon & Schuster, 1980.

Brown, Corinne, and Robert Munroe. *Time Bomb: Understanding the Threat of Nuclear Power*. New York: Morrow, 1981.

Clark, Wilson, and Jake Page. *Energy, Vulnerability and War: Alternatives for America*. New York: Norton, 1981.

Clement, Fred. *The Nuclear Regulatory Commission*. New York: Chelsea House, 1989.

Cohen, Bernard L. *Before It's Too Late: A Scientist's Case for Nuclear Energy*. New York: Plenum, 1983.

Commoner, Barry. *The Politics of Energy*. New York: Knopf, 1979.

Cuff, David J., and William J. Young. *The United States Energy Atlas*. New York: Free Press, 1980.

Department of Energy. *Annual Report*. Washington, DC: Department of Energy, 1977– .

Deudney, Daniel, and Christopher Flavin. *Renewable Energy: The Power to Choose*. New York: Norton, 1984.

Fogel, Barbara R. *Energy Choices for the Future*. New York: Franklin Watts, 1985.

Oatman, Eric F., ed. *Prospects for Energy in America*. New York: Wilson, 1980.

Teller, Edward. *Energy From Heaven and Earth*. San Francisco: W.H. Freeman, 1979.

INDEX

Catherine T. Tuggle, a native of Miami, Florida, received her education at the University of North Florida and holds master's degrees in history from both the University of Tennessee and Johns Hopkins University. She is a free-lance writer and editor as well as full-time business manager and translator for the DAR Museum at Constitution Hall in Washington, D.C.

Gary E. Weir, a native of New York City, received his B.A. from Manhattan College and his Ph.D. in history from the University of Tennessee. After a year on the history faculty at the United States Naval Academy, in 1987 he joined the newly established Contemporary History Branch of the Naval Historical Center at the Washington Navy Yard. His work on the history of naval-industrial relations in Germany and America has appeared in *Military Affairs*, *International History Review*, and *Naval Engineers Journal*.

Arthur M. Schlesinger, jr., served in the White House as special assistant to Presidents Kennedy and Johnson. He is the author of numerous acclaimed works in American history and has twice been awarded the Pulitzer Prize. He taught history at Harvard College for many years and is currently Albert Schweitzer Professor of the Humanities at the City College of New York.

PICTURE CREDITS